# THE
# AUTOBIOGRAPHY OF SHAKESPEARE

# THE
# AUTOBIOGRAPHY
## OF
# SHAKESPEARE

## A FRAGMENT

" . . . *the touch of a vanished hand,*
*And the sound of a voice that is still.*"

EDITED BY

## LOUIS C. ALEXANDER

KENNIKAT PRESS
Port Washington, N. Y./London

## NOTE.

All the footnotes are by the Editor.

THE AUTOBIOGRAPHY OF SHAKESPEARE

First published in 1911
Reissued in 1970 by Kennikat Press
Library of Congress Catalog Card No: 70-113361
ISBN 0-8046-1006-1

Manufactured by Taylor Publishing Company     Dallas, Texas

"  .  .  .  we hope, to your divers capacities, you will find enough both to draw, and hold you : for his wit could no more lie hid, than it could be lost.  Read him, therefore ; and again, and again : and then if you do not like him, surely you are in some manifest danger, not to understand him.  And so we leave you to other of his friends whom, if you need, can be your guides : if you need them not, you can lead yourselves, and others.  And such readers we wish him."

*From the Address, by John Heminge and Henrie Condell, prefixed to the First Folio Edition of Shakespeare's Works, 1623.*

"   .   .   .   Look  how  the  father's  face
Lives  in  his  issue,  even  so,  the  race
Of  Shakespeare's  mind  and  manners  brightly  shines—"

*Ben  Jonson*,  1623.

# INTRODUCTION.

FIVE years ago I laid these following papers aside. I was then much broken in health and spirit. And I was overwhelmed by the solemn importance of the work, and bewildered and almost discouraged by the many inconsistencies with known or, rather, assumed facts or beliefs, and even, very often, with itself.

Furthermore, doubts of various kinds—perhaps I should rather say subtle cross-questionings and wonderings—at times assailed me : but I had only to read some pages, almost at random, when doubt would vanish like mist before the sun.

About six months ago I was strongly impelled to complete my obvious duty. At my age of seventy-two I cannot afford further delays or daring triflings with time.

Yet I would fain have waited for further corroborations—personal, literary, topographical. I earnestly beg all who can help—particularly as regards the sermons, plays and books which

Shakespeare brought to London—to communicate with me.

I have for some months past occupied myself very perseveringly to verify and confirm, so far as possible, the statements of this momentous though broken and unrevised autobiography.

I have been ably assisted, and I have had a certain success—not very much, but strangely remarkable.

Not a word, however, have I added to my texts of 1905.

In the course of those readings, searches, correspondence, etc., I, some months ago, for the first time encountered a legend or speculation that in the year 1910 some greater light would be thrown on this deathless subject. In so far as I am consciously concerned it is a simple coincidence or accident, as it is termed—quaintly interesting, but, in my view, not otherwise noteworthy.

I now give this work to the world integrally, without a word of my own.

Here and there, I had to supply an obviously dropped letter. I have omitted some draft play-bills, and I have dealt discreetly with some words, and with some lines of confused repetition without any importance, and which would have necessitated inordinate notes to make clear.

I have also fitted in, so to speak, two detached portions at what I thought was a suitable place, relating to the arrival and earlier life in London.

Beyond these trifling and merely clerical points, and some punctuation, I have not altered, nor shaped, nor endeavoured to harmonise or reconcile with accepted versions, or to attenuate patent variances.   Indeed, so anxious am I to be an impartial and faithful editor that I will here set out briefly some of the more striking personal matters which are generally received—thus emphasising the differences.

For the sake of clearness I will, for the moment, designate the poet as Shakespeare, and another William Shakespeare whom I have to mention as simply William—using the modern spelling.

All acknowledged biographers and writers assume that Shakespeare was the son of John of Stratford-on-Avon, who was " probably a son of Richard of Snettisfield."

There is a baptismal registration of William, the son of John, and there is the record of the administration of the affairs of Richard by John.

Here the cleavage begins.

The son of John was not William Shakespeare the Poet, but William who became the wastrel and poacher and stroller and soldier.

He it was who was the " oft whipt and sometimes imprisoned " as Archdeacon Davies wrote, late in the seventeenth century, and who " was given to much unluckiness in stealing venison and rabbits."

He did worse.

For he was the reckless or besotted youth who, in his cups, or for money, or vanity, or desperation, or because he intended to go and fight in the Low Countries, was enticed into the matrimonial contract with Anne or Agnes Hathaway.

It was desirable to save appearances and to avert further scandalous disclosure : and so the young scape-grace was made to serve the purpose.

Consider this episode for an instant.

The matrimonial contract was entered into in November, 1582—a few months after her father's death ; her child was baptised in April, 1583, between four and five months later.

At the date of that contract she, being then about twenty-five, was some four or five months advanced in pregnancy : and he, even then, was only about seventeen-and-a-half years old.  She had two more children, twins, in 1585.

Moreover, there has not been found any proof, or even assertion, that the contemplated marriage of William and Anne was ever solemnised.

But this *complaisant,* or else most precocious profligate, this " oft whipt and sometimes imprisoned," was not the Poet, but his cousin.

" The suggestion that he joined, at the end of 1585, a band of youths of the district for serving in the Low Countries under the Earl of Leicester, whose Castle of Kenilworth was within easy reach of Stratford-on-Avon, was based on the obvious confusion between him and others of his name."*

I agree.

It was not Shakespeare, but William the son of John, his cousin, who became the soldier.

The poet was the son of Richard of Warwick, who was the son of Thomas of that town.  This Thomas Little, or Thomas the Little, who later took the name of Shakespeare, was the son-in-law of John of Warwick, and the brother-in-law of Richard of Snettisfield.

* Sidney Lee.

There were then not a few other Richards Shakespeare. In Rowington alone, twelve miles north of Stratford, in the same Hundred, there were three, each having a son named William ; and another at Wroxhall.

There was a William who was drowned in the Avon in 1579.

On the day preceding the registration of the matrimonial contract of William and Anne—viz., on the 27th of November, 1582, there is recorded in the registry of the Bishop of Worcester the matrimonial contract of a William Shakespeare and Anne Whatley :—two Williams on two successive days.

William, the son of John, is said to have died of a fever about 1589—being then a soldier.

Shakespeare, who is stated by biographers to have probably been a "schoolmaster in his early years " became an under-usher in a country school ; and, some four years later, he went to an uncle in London, who died soon after. It was some years further that he married his "pretty cousine Anne Hathaway," who was evidently a very winsome woman though, it must be regretfully confessed, frail and false as fair, not the wife he ought to have married—or that she ought to have been. She was then contractually free; actually, that is ecclesiastically, married she had not been.

He dealt liberally with her surviving children, the daughters, in his Will—his own child having presumably died—although he had, too late, discovered much regarding his wife, to whom he bequeathed in an interlined and, maybe, ironic afterthought his "second-best bedstead," and its belongings.

It is certain that he intended to *revise*, but it never came to this. That intention may, perhaps, account for the apparent carelessness with which names were set down, as it were, provisionally— especially those of leading actors and theatrical proprietors ; and probably also as to dates, places and other things.

It is most strange that he should veil the names of those distinguished actors—the Burbages, Heminge, Condell,—and employ such as Sholton, Prentiss, Sellieres, (a name given in his list of books) Albertus* and others; whilst the names of

---

* There was the Oxford Regius Professor of Civil Law, the friend of Sir Philip Sydney, Albericus Gentilis, who published that great and ponderous work De Jure Belli (1588-1598). Whether the name Albericus suggested Albertus, I do not know. The satire is as blunt as the playfulness now.—Albertus Magnus and Albertinus Rubeus were of 100 years earlier.

some minor actors—particularly of some who impersonated female parts, as he himself did until he became an author—are correctly given, as I have been able to verify.

Somewhat—perhaps, much—may be fairly attributed to transcriber's, officious prompters, interrupters; and errors are very apt to arise from haste, confusion, misunderstanding, moods, mockings, imperfections of memory, sly humours and the like.

I ask myself—Was this so—the outcome of a wit or of a whimsicality now painfully flat, an allusiveness to which I have no sure key, the careless rough-hewing in view of later shaping? Or is the awful overhanging thought correct that there was some partial unbalancing of his majestic mind by his poignant domestic griefs and dishonours working on such a nature as his?

I can only surmise—I cannot explain; more light may come. My business here simply is to edit, and not to speculate or discuss.

That revision, had it been made, would have done so much—for it would doubtless also have carried the work further.

Readers may see some facts and dates which conflict with those which are, or which are considered to be, established; and they may even prove the correctness of the latter over against the former.

They are, however, requested to remember that they have here presented to them only unrevised drafts; also that I am quite aware, by my recent readings and searchings, of what has been otherwise said and believed. It had been very easy to avoid or avert comparisons, or to propitiate criticism of a certain kind, if mere harmony or symmetry were desired—at the price of truth. Nor do I ignore what, at times, seems so like eccentricity or heedlessness.

Readers may be incredulous at first—that is but natural; but let them not be impatient or scornful or hasty, or flippant—that most vulgar form of affected smartness; the cheap mark of ignorance, indolence and impertinence.

Let them the rather read the rest—even apart from the historical framework, so to speak—if only as literature, pure and simple; for this is no ordinary book. And to those who may write thereon I would say—If you respect truth and your vocation, and yourself—read it *through* first, slowly and conscientiously.

Can anyone mistake the inimitable voice of Shakespeare?

I intend to prepare a small book bearing upon this, in which I may also give some pages of extraordinary related interest : and I cherish the hope that I may be permitted to have the entire vouchsafed fragment—for so I must call it, considerable though it be—reproduced in *facsimile*, as well as the other pieces which I indicate.

I trust, by the co-operation of readers, to secure yet further verifications—not for my own satisfaction, of course, but for that of others—and to work out some clues of a somewhat mixed but very significant nature.

But, whilst much—in the matter of names, dates and circumstances—remains to be disentangled and cleared up, so far as may now be possible—the glorious text speaks for itself.

L. C. ALEXANDER.

Holly Lodge,
　　Putney, S.W.
　　*12th December*, 1910.

# THE AUTOBIOGRAPHY OF SHAKESPEARE.

## A FRAGMENT.

I WAS born in the City of Warwicke, and my father's name was Richard. His father's name was Thomas Little, and he changed the name of Little to Shakspere on the entreaty of my grandmother's father, John Shakspere of Warwicke.

He was a Hollander, born at Utrecht, and was a small man of many parts—a ripe scholar, and philosopher, and lover of books.

I remember my father, Richard Shakspere of Warwicke. He was a small dark man, and had a large head and very little hands and feet, being as to that like my grandfather, Thomas of Utrecht, as I was often told.

He was a very indolent man—not learned, nor given to books, but, at the same time, not liking any business or work or cares of any kind, but the rather being disposed and given to argument and laughter and novelties and curiosities of all kinds. Had it not been for my Uncle John, of Stratford-on-Avon, my father's business had long since gone to waste and ruin ; and even as it was he did mightily neglect it, and made light of losses, and was fooled and chicaned and deceived on every side—the which he took, as he said, like a philosopher, and as every one else said like a ninny.

My mother had a sharp tongue, but she could never mend him.

He loved us—my younger brother John and me—but he often seemed as if we were not living, or loving him ; though at times he would play with us, and tell us stories, and sing to us, and buy us sweetmeats and toyes.

I was but a very little boy but I mind me well of him, and of his fantastic way of curling his moustachios and beard—which were dark and shining, as were his fine large eyes—very unlike the hue and complexion of the Shaksperes of Warwicke and Stratford-on-Avon and of other parts whom I did in after years meet, which were light and somewhat inclined to auburn or red.

My father had a very fine voice and could sing most ravishingly, and often his neighbours would come in and press him to sing, and faith ! not much pressing did he need, for he greatly delighted therein and was very proud thereof. Also, he accompanied himself, when he listed, on the harpsichord, of which he had bought not less than two, though they cost him a matter of over fifteen pounds each, at the which extravagance all the town did laugh, and my mother was distraught with fury ; but not a damn cared he.

I remember some songs he was wont to sing :

The love of Sir Lewis Landes
The Cross of St. Salvador.
The Knight of Ayre.
My love she went a-maying.
I will not brook a knave.
Here's to the Lady of my Heart.
When I was young and gay.
Madame, I am Sir Lollilop.
The Stolen Kisses of Sir Bernard.
The   .   .   .

and others that I do now forget.

He also did make some ballades and set the tunes

to some of them, and he was often bidden to feastes and weddings and other joyous gatherings ; and he was, altogether, a bright and shiftless soul, always ready to neglect his own affaires and to help anybody else's, in the which he took more concernes and pains than ever he did show in his own.

My mother was not of a happy disposition, and never was she pleased with my father whom she for ever rated and called him English names—by the which I mean to say such words as Lazybones, and Wastrel, and Vagabond, and Ballademonger, and the like—which made him laugh at times, and very furious and bad-tempered at other times ; and then I would weep or creep away, and think that I would like to die and be out of this terrible hurly-burly and sore, troublous, and perplexed home.

When my father died of a pleurisy my Uncle John of Stratford-on-Avon he did take our affaires in hand, and took me and my brother John to live with him for that my mother could not keep us by reason of her being soon to be married to one Master Stockley, a brutal man and a butcher of Warwicke—the which haste and marriage was monstrously displeasing to my Uncle, and, as I learned after, to all other of my relations. My Uncle carried on the business for a time, and I know not to a certainty what did happen, for there were many quarrels and disputes with my mother over the said Stockley even before their hated marriage, and I know not what other clamours and differences.

We never did see our mother after Uncle John did take us with him to his home until she died, when the man Stockley did relent and allow my mother for to see us as she was a-dying. But he got drunk, and did insult my Uncle John, and they fought together, and my Uncle John did bestow upon him a mighty and most God-blessed beatinge for the which he was like to die also—but he recovered in about two or three weekes' time, and his wife, my mother, was buried and the man Stockley could not by reason of his hurts follow the coffin to the grave, nor appear to any of the company ; and not a man nor a woman in Warwicke was there who did not rejoice in his drubbing.

I mind me with most fervent remembrance and unfeigned joy of a great old chest, which three men could not but with great labour lift into a cart,

which my Uncle John took from my father's
house when he did remove my brother and me
thereto.  That chest—ah, how often did I in after
time revere and bless and love it !  for it held a lot
of bookes that had been my grandfather's, and
sheaves and stacks, so to speak, of papers written
by him and which, later, I did most eagerly
devour, and bask in, and glory in, and bathe in,
and swim, and fly as it were on angels' wings to
lands and realms of peace and philosophy and
faerie and romance.

Beloved Ancestor—Great though Little Thomas !
Who didst fly on pinions of the mind to lands
Unknown to men of baser mode and lower nature ;
And didst perceive, as with a wizard's eye, the
Beauty and the strength that lay beyond
All human thought and reason ; and the
Wisdom and mysterious design that undershot
All the Creator's animate and inanimate Ellipse—
While that thy great heart did all embrace in love,
And thy lofty soul in lowly worship bent—
I cannot think thee gone far from me e'en now,
For I feel as if my weak hand lay still in thine,
Which in this mortal life it never touched,
And that thine eyes looke into my heart
And teach it more, much more, than there it learns,
Until, informed by thee, the blood thus sanctified

Mounts to my brain, and there enthronés thee—
Inspirer, teacher, immortal Ancestor,
Whom, by God's Grace, I may some bright day see,
And so crown all my divine felicity.

*     *     *     *     *

My father died in 1576, and I went to live with my Uncle John Shakspere of Stratford-on-Avon— I and my younger brother John, who died while I was in London.

In 1576 or 1578—I forget what I did in the time between my going to my Uncle and my going to the school—I was by him entered as a scholar at St. Saviour's, Burslem,* where I remained about four years.

I studied the humanities, and history, and I read greedily, at all times of the day and night, some of the books on all kinds of subjects that had belonged to my grandfather Thomas, and had been preserved by my father Richard. Those books were in French and English, which I could read easily, and some in Dutch and German which I could not read at all, and some in Latin which I could read only with some difficulty. There were also many writings in his hand of

* I shall, at another time, discuss the point whether Birmingham is here intended, or Alleyn's School at Stone.

comments and arguments, and some poetic pieces of not much worth, and many unfinished pieces of writing begun at odd times and in divers places, and put aside and not further proceeded with.

My grandfather was evidently a man of a fine fancy and much learning, and with a great love of solitude, and of nature, and of riddles about the world to come, and the like.

When I left St. Saviour's school I went to be an Under-Usher at Sittingbourne School, Hoddingdon*, or Hoddingley—Hoddingleigh, in the County of Warwicke.

I must set down that while I was an Under-Usher at Sittingbourne, Hoddinley, my Uncle John of Stratford-on-Avon did, when opportunity served by carrier or by any friend or neighbour going that way, send me for my use and cheer sundry matters—such as a fat duck, or a capon, or some clothing, and at times some money—two shillings belike—or a holy letter to my master for to ask his leave for me to come to him.

[A holy letter is a letter sent by a parent or guardian to a master or a teacher wherein is expressed the desire to have the pupil, or prentice, or whatever he might be, let out for a space on a holiday or a visit or the like.]

* This, likewise, I hope to identity later.

My wages as Under-Usher was twenty shillings by the quarter in addition to my keep, but my clothing and shoeing and mendings were at my own charges. I did also earn me some small sums by teaching private persons, and by translating from the French and Latin for divers people who might at times require the same, but these earnings were small as they were fitful.

I spent nearly every shilling I got in buying of bookes of which, with what my Uncle saved that were my father's come to him from my grandfather Thomas, I gathered a fair number of an infinite diversity and discursive variety, and all the which I did most ravenously devour—whether classical, or modern, or mythical, or poetical, or historical, or scientific, or travelling, or philosophical, or disputatious. In short, I spared none and browsed on all the pastures, high and low, rich and poor, dry or wet, till there was scarcely any subject but I knew some smattering thereof and could bravely talk thereon, and yet scarcely a one that I was in any way profound or well-grounded in. / My mind was like to a Venetian mosaic, and none of any consequence by itself or for its own worth, but yet the whole forming a smooth and shapely entirety, giving all beholders the spectacle of a pleasant and clever picture.

My life at Hoddingley was serene and studious. I was a singer in the Church Choir, and often I did sit with the Vicar, Sir John Stephen Thompson, M.A., and we would spend long evenings together at his house and discuss all sorts of authors and books, and controversies, and speculations. He read a many of my little poems and tales and essays, and did give me many hints and corrections. He kept many of my little writings for his pleasure and for keepsakes, at the which I was the proudest and most elated youth in the County.

I was a good fencer and loved that pastime most inordinately : also, I used to go a-fishing, and often forgot my rod and line and fish and all when the thought did take me, and I sat me down to write upon it, and would as like as not ramble away—and perhaps I would not perceive my loss until I was four or five miles away.

I became a very passable tailor in the mending of my clothes, and I did often patch my shoon, and I bought me an awl and bristles and lapstone and—bar the cutting out—I think I could become a very commendable cobbler.

I had other distractions, such as Cudgel-playing and Wrestling, for although I was small I was very strong and active ; and also Archery, and Bowls, and Chess and Chequers ; and I danced with the maids, and had my sweethearts by the score, and kissed a-many, and I thank my God I deluded not one to her downfall or ruin.

My dear Uncle John—Heaven rest his honest loving soul!——was ever very fond of me; I sometimes thought more even than any of his own children. He would often take me aside and then, when we two were alone together, would he ask me to read him my stories and translations and poems—the which I most willingly and proudly did. He would sit and listen with moving face and eye and lip like a child, and for the most time with his great arm around my shoulders.

Dear Uncle John ! Perchance, I did bring him the comfort and satisfaction which counter-availed the pains and shames which my Cousin William, his own Son, did cause him ; or maybe, it was that there were within his bosom and his mind wells and springs of thoughts and feelings unknown to all else except his Maker, and only dimly perceived of by even himself.

Wheresoever thou art, Uncle John, thy fond
and unforgetful nephew hopes that thy true and
strong and tender soul will expand and grow to
its perfect beauty, and rise to higher spheres of
life, and knowledge, and happiness.

\* \* \* \* \*

I was there until 1582 or thereabouts, when I
went to London, being thereunto invited by my
Uncle John Shakspere of Lincoln's Inn, a learned
man of the Law, but not a member of the Inn;
and I lived with him in his chambers at No. 16,
St. George's Street, in the Borough of Southwark. He was a bachelor, and very poor, but he
worked hard and earned enough to keep us living;
but he died shortly after, and I was left in London
almost destitute.

\* \* \* \* \*

I brought with me to London when I came up
from Hoddingley about thirty or more of my
books, the which I prized above all else in the
world. They were as I remember full well:

Plutarch's Lives of Eminent men.
Virgil's Enead and His Eclogues.
Stoneman's Episodes and Scenes of Italian Life in
1400 to 1500.

Bellaires, His Travels in Italy.

Thomas Stephenson, his Sonnets.

Thomas Stephenson, his Sonnets.  No. 2.

Ellis Paine, his Showman's Guide.

John Elias Ellis, his Romance of the Seven Kings.

The History of Greece by Simeon Levi of Paris in French.

The History of Rome by the Brothers Silver (The Goldsmiths of Cornhill).

The Poems of Anthony Stone of Sevenoaks in Kent.

The Life and Times of Alexander the Great.

The Mirror of Beauty and Fame, by several Authors in a sort of Miscellany.

The History of Greece by Stephenson and abridged by him for Scholars.

The Epics of Hypocrites, and Ovid's Odes, in one binding.

The Tragedies of Euripedes and Sophocles in French Translations by Monsieur Antoine Genelon (or Fenelon).

The Plays of The Good Woman, The Long Lane that Hath no Turning, The Bridge of Sighs, The Serpent on the Hearth, The Stony Heart, The Stonemason's Daughter, The Bluebell of Scotland, The Merry Tale of Antony and the Pig, The Ghost, The Shadow on the Wall, The Slain Boar of Arden, The Stain on the Stair, The Thorn in the Heel, The Thorn in the Flesh, The Jew of York, The Stone in the Sling, The Lazy Man of Aldeborough, The Lost Pearl, The Lost Will, The Lost Link, The Silent Sleepers of Ceylon,

The Wreck of the St. George, The Stupid Boy, The Sailor's Wife, The Sailor's Home on the Seas, The Smuggler's Cave, The Smugglers of Colvey, The Brothers, The Moor, The Welcome Guest, The Great Lot of Gold, The Yelling of a Fool, The Poor Girl of London Town, The Elixir of Life, The Miser of Maidstone Town, The Collection of Simeon Levy's French——, The Law and the Lady, The Lawyer's Fee, The Lawyer's Soul, The Steel Sword of Achilles, The Way of the World, The last of the Show, The Silver Bowl, The Whore, The Fairy Dance, The Lovers of Arles, The Standard, Bearer's Brand, The Bold Outlaw, The Slow and Sure, The Longest Day, The Death of a Slowbody, The Robbers of the Hills, The Seven Sleepers, The Lady of Llewelyn's Tower, The Shrew of Shrewsbury, The Shrew's Husband, The Terrace of Flowers, The Tragedy of the Sea, The Marriage of a Beggar, The Rider of Winchester, The Theatre of Shows and Comedies,

and a number of minor things of that sort—the whole made up and bound in six fair volumes in stout calf ; the which had cost me many a loss of supper, and work o' nights, and scraping and paring, for to get the wherewithal to buy from one Master John Wilkes of Hoddingley, who solde them to me, after great bargaininges, for the sum of Forty shillings, the which I did pay him piecemeal as I was able.

Seutonius.

The History of England, in Two Volumes, by Robert A-Thomas, the Doctor of Hereford and Canon of St. Paul's.

The Letters of a Son to his Father, by Stephen Browne.

The Victories of the Soul, by Thomas Severn.

The Eel Fishers, by Master Elias Severn.

The Stories of the Ladies of Paris, by Monsieur A. Sellières, in French.

The Emperor of Germany, His History, by Alexander* Goldinge.

The Emperor of Germany, His Wars and Conquests, by Alexander Goldinge.

The Sultan of Turkey, His Life and Wives and Slaves, by Antoine Genelon (or Fenelon) in French.

The Marquis of Bath, a Poem by Samuel Robins.

The Elements of Latin and Greek, by Stephen Browne.

The Book of Proverbs and the Holy Gospels and my Book of Common Prayer.

The Old Testament in a black leather bindinge.

The Old Last Words of a Christian, by Alexander Goldinge.

The Songs and Ballads of old England, by Master Alfred Selby of Selby, Yorks.

The Glossary of Greek and Latin Phrases, by Stephen Browne.

* This name should be " Arthur." The initial only was most frequently used.

The Silver Thread to Learning, by Samuel Robins.

Poems of Hesiod and Aristophanes, translated by Stephen Browne.

(I call them Poems* rather than Dramatists because I think that there is no real portraiture of human life and action, as we do perceive and conceive of it, but rather parable, and symbol, and presentations suited to their times. What may fitly have been deemed dramatic then is now more fitly denominated poetical only.)

The Lessons in Latin and English, and Greek and English, by Stephen Browne.

The Lights and Shades of a Woman's Life, by Alexander Goldinge.

The Sorrows of a Man of Mark, by the same.

The Way of Sin and Sinners, by Master John Hope.†

The Thorney Path of Youth, by the same.

The Solitary, by the same.

The Selfish Man, by the same.

The Stolen Belt, by the same.

The Churchgoer's Aid to Devotion, by Master J. Hope.

The Saintly Life of St. Francis, by the same.

The Soul and the Body, by the same.

The Soul's delight in God, by the same.

---

* " Poems rather than Dramatists " (*sic*) an obvious grammatical slip.

† This, and the twelve succeeding sermons were probably in one or two volumes. The author, John Hope, was most likely Bishop John Hooper, whose name was also printed, at times, as John Hoper.

The Wicked and his Fate, by the same.
The Old, Old, Story, by the same.
The Still, Still Voice, by the same.
The Sweet Lot, by the same.
The Elves of English Dales, by Master George Hutchinges.
The Fairy Tales of England, by the same.
The Songs of England, by the same.

There were some more the names of which abide no longer in my memory ; but there was not one that was not a friend, and that had not cost me much in thought, and in sacrifice in meals, and better clothes, and games, and labour ; and when I did survey my so great treasures I did afterwards marvel that I could have gotten them all by honest means with my so slender ones.

These brought I to London with me, and I took up my abode, on my Uncle's commendation, in a lodging at Mistress Hennessey or Hersey, a widow woman, No̱  in Grays Inn Lane, hard by to where stood an Inn called the Lamb Inn, at the corner of Gray's Inn Lane and the Inn of Court of Gray's Inn.

She gave me a chamber at the top of her house with a great belly of a window with many tiny squares of panes therein, the which looked out on the gardens of the Inns of Court, which did mightily please me, and I was to pay her by the weeke two shillings.

I had brought with me also some apparel, and sundry other belongings—such as a cross-bow, and single sticks, and quoits, and the like ; and while that my Uncle lived I could make ado and shift for to pay her and to live—or, rather, to exist.

But when he died I did suffer most dire distresses for I had no money, and I could finde no worke whereby I might earne some.

I had to sell my things for to get bread to eat.

I sold my cross-bow and the sticks and quoits and other the like objects whereby I got three shillings and fourpence ; and when that was all spent my real woes began in very truth and bitterness. I had to sell my bookes . . . !

My fond bookes—every one a child—a brother —bone of my bone, blood of my blood, heart of my heart.

How shall I tell what I then did endure—how describe my tears, my anguish, my complaints to the cruel bereaving niggardly Heavens—my desires for death—my orphaned and despoiled rebellions and desolations of soul. . . . . .

for I wanted help, and found none ; and I wished
for work, and could get none ; and all the world
seemed to care not for me, nor what would become
of me ; and I would fain have had it whelmed in
one vast destruction in which I, too, had been
extinguished, by clutching my dear bookes as
Samson held fast by the pillars.

But hunger in the end prevailed.

Oh, I was like a traitor who betrayed his
dearest friend.   I was like a denatured father
who thrust out his tenderest children.   I was
as an ingrate, and a barbarian, and a callous
monster.

I spoke to them, and did reason with them,
and excused my base acts, and begged their
forgiveness, and kissed them ere I parted from
them ; and as Hagar moved away that she might
not see her fond child die so I ran from the shops
where I had so ruthlessly, but alas ! so necessi-
tously, abandoned my dear bookes : and thereafter
avoid passing thereto, but the rather made longe
tours and windings so as not to pass the place
again, to avoid—not the sore memory, for that I
ever carried with me, but—the anguishes of their
reproachings in case I saw them, and the hot and

unavailing angers and jealousies in case I saw them handled or bought by other men.

So, one by one—or set by set—I did sell my bookes, and while I fed my frame—and most sparely, too—I did bleed and drain as 'twere my life's best blood ; and I wonder now less how I lived but the rather why I did give my coward consent to live at such untellable cost of wordless torment.

It was Providence that did sustain me through that bitter time. Perchance, too, it was a teaching and a discipline for me—though a most exquisite and refined pain. The remembrance of those days swells my bosom and fills mine eyes with pity of the poor, tortured, unfriended, helpless youth —though I know that youth was I—e'en I myself.

I have sometimes thought, when recalling some of those galling recollections, that we men are blind, and less sapient than the lower creatures in many ways. We fail before our misfortunes and we have scarcely the courage, much less the sagacity, to look beyond them and see in the scourgings of To-day the healings, and even the greater beautifyings of the Morrow. We are apt to consider each of them as a crisis or as a catastrophe when, in truth, it is but a surpassing tangle, or an accidental knot, or ravelling of the silken cord on which our lives—the precious pearls of God—are strung. The pain is very real in the enduring, and the consolations of religion are oftimes absent, and the arguments of philosophy are most unsatisfying, even if they come not too late ; and 'tis only in the retrospection that the true harmonies, and the sweet uses of the cruel-seeming mercies, became apparent to us.

To me at that time—hungry, friendless desperate, in a town where I beheld so much of careless wealth and pleasure, of fulness and fatness of living, and contentment and jollity and cheer, and of kinships and comradeships, and of lovemaking and laughter, and all the fulsome clamour of life and its movements and thousand-sided manifestations—what could Religion have whispered, or what could Philosophy have argued, to reconcile me to my hard fate ?

For, look you, I was yet scarce a man—a country lad in London, without a penny and without a friend, and unable to find that which should earn him e'en a crust.

Yet was Providence most kind, for thus it

schooled me, in timely hour, for the still harder
ordeals which lay before me.* I was but poorly
tempered in those forges at the best—but somewhat was I yet hardened.

And when, in after years, I tasted what it was
to be in comfort and renown, I began to see that the
sluices of the water-ways of our lives may run dry
at times, or be exceeding low, but 'tis only that
the lower locks be the better filled.

* * * * *

I tried to learn how to play the flute and gain
a little money, but I failed. Then I tried to teach,
but I likewise failed. I then tried to get employment as a player in a company, as I remembered
hearing that my Cousin William had done ; and
at length, after many weary efforts, and much
suffering and penury, even to the going hungry
and bedless at nights, I found employ with one
Johanne Sholton of Bridewell, Blackfriars, who
then had a theatre called the Palatine Theatre.

He hired me to play some women's parts, such
as Rebecca in Sholton's own piece of Rebecca

---

* " Still harder ordeals." He gained fame and wealth, troops of
friends, honours and the magnificent consciousness of genius. What
was that most bitter drop in the over-brimming cup ? I answer without
hesitation—his infamous wife.

and the  .  .  .  and of Stella in Sholton's own piece of the Prince of Denmark, and of Emma in his piece of Emma the forgotten child of  .  .  . and others similar to these, for the which he paid me one pound or one pound four shillings by the week, whereat I was very contented.

I stayed with him about a year or a year and a half, and then I went and hired myself to one Edward Lockyer or Lockhard, or some such name, at the Westminster Theatre in Slowe Street, near to the old house where lived one Charles Stevens, a man of great parts, who wrote plays and acted in them.

I stayed with Lockhar, or Lockyer, for about a year, and then I left him and hired myself to one Master Samuel Phipps of the Theatre of St. Martin's Lane called the Princes Theatre.

While I was with Lockyer I played such parts as Emma in Sholton's piece, and Emily in the other piece of his, and Mary of Sloven Hall, and Ellen of the Mill, and Stephonia of the piece called the Queen of Sheba, and others of the like.  He paid to me about one pound or one pound four shillings by the week.  We played every night except Sunday, and, at times, before the Queen, and the

Nobility, and the Quality in Town, for the which I was paid extra—about two shillings or two shillings and fourpence each performance.

When I went to the Westminster Theatre I was to have better payment—about one pound ten or twelve shillings by the week—but it fell out otherwise, for Master Sholton he brought suit and action against Master Lockyer, and he won the same, and Master Lockyer had to pay him divers damages and charges, and there was interdiction of the playing of his plays or of imitating of them; and so Master Phipps was fain to shut up his Theatre, for he had a partnership with Master Lockyer—and I was left without employment and without money, and was at my wit's end how to live.

I had become acquainted with several persons, notably one Stephen* England and one Edward England, his brother, both honest men and good fellows who took me into their house at No. 24 Elle Street—Elbe Street, and I stayed with them, while looking for employ, or service, or any way whereby I might earn my livelihood. They were booksellers and they knew of my love for books,

* John.

and they made me free of their stores so far as I had time for reading.  I stayed with them for about a month, when I got employ with Master Samuel Phipps once more—this time at his Theatre at Islington called the Royal Islington Theatre.

I played there in such parts as Susannah, in Susannah and the Elders, and Emily—as he had made his peace with Sholton—and Emma, for the like reason, and others of the like sort.  He paid me about eighteen shillings by the week, and I was well content after my privations for the past few weeks.  I remained with him there about six months when I left to go to Master John Dane of the Norwich Theatre Royal of Norwich.

I stayed at Norwich, and in travelling about the Eastern Counties, about six months, and I was paid about one pound ten or twelve shillings by the week, and I saved about eight pounds—and felt that I was a rich man and likely to die of wealth.

I then returned to London, and being no longer in want, I set myself to think why I should not write a piece like Sholton who was making much money, and was run after for the liberty to perform his pieces, for the which he received goodly payment without any labour or trouble. Moreover, I thought that his pieces were miserable and poor, and often silly, and never bright or sound. I thought much, and walked about a good deal in the Park, and in the fields about Marylebone, and the lanes of Hampstead. I was then lodging with a Mistress Jane George of No. 20—No. 60.— I forget the number—Alpine Lane in the Borough of Southwark, near to St. George's Church.

After much thought, and the planning out of my plots and designs, I remembered some of the books of my grandfather, and some of the little stories that I had myself written when I was a scholar at St. Saviour's, Burslem ; and at length, after much cogitation, and the forming of many English plays, I decided myself to write a play on the subject of Stephen, King of England, in three acts and a number of scenes.

I began this play in September 1585* and worked upon it for many days and nights, and at last it was finished, and I took it to Master Sholton— who would not even look at it ; and I fared no better with Master Phipps ; and Master Lockyer

* See note relating to the first production of " The Tempest."

laughed in my face and said—Thou beardless jackanapes. Go, and get thee a letter for Bedlam —and the like sweet encouragement did I receive.

So I went home, and took my piece which had cost me so much pain and labour, and so many headaches and tears—for I did use to weep for the creatures whom my fancy created—and I tore it into pieces, and I burnt it to the very last shred of paper, and then I went out and resolved to drown myself in the River Thames and have done with it—so tired and broken in heart and spirit was I at these ill turns of fate.

I walked about that evening, waiting until the people shall have gone home and the streets be dark, and nobody to see or hinder me, for I was sick, and despairing, and wounded in my pride.

And as I walked—and disdained even to pray, so bitter was my heart—I became aware of something like a slow lightening of my mind, as if someone approaching a dark passage with a candle yet still far off, albeit the light was heralding its own coming, and I was feeling almost angry because my mood was getting little by little somewhat gayer, and more serene and tolerant of misfortune, and hopeful for my life.

I stopped to question myself and what all these contradictions within the small compass of one man's nature might mean, and as I thought, came memories of things that I had read, especially in my grandfather Thomas' writings, or scraps and fragments of writings, which would to God he had finished and left as precious gifts to the world !— for he was a rare man and lofty spirit, though his stature was small, and his origin outlandish, but none the worse for that.

And with the memories came reflections, and whisperings of life, as well as reminders of the wise and high things that came back swiftly into my memory, until, at the last, I stood still at Thames-side, near where the Fleet reaches unto it, and I cast my eyes to the starry heavens, and I cried to God to forgive me my petulance and impatience, and want of faith in Him, the Father of all His creatures.

Ease of mind—even cheerfulness—even gaiety —even joy seemed to pour into my heart as wine is poured into a bottle through a filler until it is full to overflowing ; and I walked away from the darkly-flowing river and up into Fleet Street, and I fumbled in my fob for some forlorn shillings that still lay there, and I went into the Owl Tavern that then stood close to St. Bride's Church near Bridewell, and did there sup and drink like a prince, and thereafter I walked home to my lodgings—and it seemed as if I walked on the air, for my heart was light although my pocket was well-nigh empty.

I did not mourn the loss of Stephen the King, for I was filled, not with bare hope alone, though sweet and vital and divine it be, but also with courage and confidence.

I thanked God on my knees that night that He had vouchsafed to intervene to hold me back from destruction, and I felt the more convinced that I had to live, and that my life would be of use—perchance of value—to others as to myself.

I slept well, and on the next morning I, as if I were become a different and older, and an experienced and critical person, considered and, in the main, condemned my play of Stephen the King, and wondered how I could ever think it even a passable piece in many parts thereof. I almost wondered how, with my knowledge of stagecraft, I could have written it, and I almost felt my face grow red, though I was all alone, when I thought

of its being played before people.  I was thankful
that it was no more.  Then I laughed as I considered that it was barely fifteen hours since I
thought that I was doing murder when I burnt it,
and yet I was weighing and judging it as if I was
fifteen years older since I had written it.

I took a paper and wrote on the top of a
page

## THE TEMPEST

### A COMEDY BY WILLIAM SHAKSPERE.

I had had the idea long before in various forms
of treatment.

I at once began to work, and I laboured incessantly for about four months, supporting myself
the while by playing occasionally at Greenwich and
other places ; and my landlady, Mrs. George, was
a kindly soul, and never pressed me for money,
but, on the contrary, she would often come to my
room and set food and drink before me, and almost
compel me to eat, for I was so intent upon my
work that often would I forget to do so.

When my play was finished I went and conferred
with my good friends John and Edward England,
and they advised me to sell it to Sholton or some

other Proprietor of a Playhouse.   So I went to him
and he would have none of it or of me.

Then I went to Master Phipps, who said the same
thing to me.

Then I went to Master Lockyer who likewise told
me to go and get myself hanged.

Then John England said to me—

" William, thy luck is not with those men.
They are asses and mules and self-conceited
knaves.   Come with me, and we shall see what
we can do in spite of them."

So we went, and conferred for several days, at
the end whereof we took a decision to take a house
ourselves and make a playhouse thereof, the which
we did forthwith ; and the two Englands, with
some friends of theirs and some friends of mine,
found some money and took a house in Blackfriars Road near to the street called —— a street
that runs off into another street called Silver
Street I think and on the 8th day of March 1588,*
we opened with my play of the Tempest.

It was a great success.

The parts were played—so far as I remember
thus :—

* I propose to deal elsewhere with the subject of dates, generally.

| Prospero | .. | .. | Mr. Albertus. |
|---|---|---|---|
| Ferdinand | .. | .. | Mr. Sinclaire. |
| The Duke | .. | .. | Mr. Frein. |
| Trinculo | .. | .. | Mr. Andrew—— |
| Sebastian | .. | .. | Mr. John Edmund—— |
| Caliban | .. | .. | Myself. |
| Ariel | .. | .. | Master Edwin Stocks. |
| Miranda | .. | .. | Mr. Elvaston. |

We played the piece for nearly two months, and all the Town came to see it, and we made a profit of nearly two hundred pounds when and whatsoever the charges and expenses had been paid and acquitted.

I received as my share, apart from my pay as a player of the part of Caliban, the sum of over one hundred pounds.

My fortune was made, and my name was in all men's mouths, for all said and declared that it was a famous play ; and the Queen herself did send for me, and we performed in her Grace's presence at Windsor on the 18th day of October 1588, for the which she gave us twenty pounds, and she gave me leave to kiss her hand, the which I dutifully did, and felt mightily honoured by the doing.

After this piece we played other pieces, but we

did not make much gain by them, so that I was easily persuaded to begin another play, which I did at the end of 1588—being then lodged near the Theatre at a house in Blackfriars Road No. — kept by a man named —— a man employed in the Theatre. The house was hard by to an Inn called the Plough Inn kept by one named Perkins, a very fat man with a very slim wife, and we used to call them Thick-and-thin.

My second play was called

## THE MERRY STORY OF OLDCASTLE,

but I changed the title to the

## MERRY WIVES OF WINDSOR,

because Oldcastle was the name of a very honourable family, and I did not wish to give them any pain or annoyance. I used the name Falstaff instead in the play.

No,—it is not true that I had written some historical plays at that time in which Falstaff had appeared, and that the Queen had asked me to write a play in which the merry Knight should be made to fall in love.

That is all fancy and fable.

I had not at that time written any plays except the Tempest—not counting Stephen, which was dead and damned—at least encinderated.

I finished the Merry Wives of Windsor in about two months, and we performed it for the first time in our theatre on the fourth day of March 1589. The cast was—as well as I can remember—as follows :—

| | | |
|---|---|---|
| Falstaff | .. .. | Mr. Perkins. |
| Master Groom | .. .. | „ Brown. |
| Sir | .. .. .. | |
| Mistress Groom | .. .. | Master Chase. |
| Mistress Page | .. .. | Master —— |
| Anne Page | .. .. | Master Elwood. |
| Mistress Blood | .. | Master Stewart. |
| Mistress Cloudley | .. | Master Stephens. |
| Mistress Sloven | .. .. | Master Hollies. |
| Fairies, Elves, etc., etc., etc. | | |

Sir—plague on't ! I can't bring his name to mind ; 'tis the Welsh parson in love with Anne Page: and there is also the part of the husband of Mistress Page, and of Mistress Flood (not Blood) and also that of another man—he who personates the Knight at the basket, and the Knight's servant, one Bardolph.

I have them somewhat confused in my memory, but I doubt not I shall remember them all again more truly anon.

I took the part of Master Slender—that is a name I sought so hard and could not reach unto —but I played only for a few nights because I did not do it well, as I was not accustomed to male impersonations, and this was my first effort in that direction. The part was given to one Jenkyns, a man from Wales as he said, but I thought him an Irishman.

I played no more in that piece, but I altered it many times and reduced its volume a good deal.

The piece took the populace and the Quality mightily, and we did make much profit; and the Queen commanded us to perform it before her Grace two times—once at Windsor on the 3rd day of September 1589, and once at Greenwich on the 7th of day October 1589—for the which she gave us twenty pounds on each occasion, and gave me leave to kiss her Royal hand, the which I did most dutifully and gratefully, being highly honoured by her in the so permitting me.

At the end of four months we ceased to perform this play, and we found that we had made a clear gain of over three hundred and thirty pounds, whereof there fell to me, as my share, the huge sum of one hundred and sixty pounds.

There were proper instruments of contract between the Englands and me and other parties, the which were drawn by one Master Shollance of No. 8, Mitre Court out of Fleet Street, an attorney, and for the which we paid him jointly divers sommes of about three pounds and some shillings in all. The said instruments of contract were kept by him for the use and benefit and convenience of all the parties, and they were never removed from his handes but lay there, for they never were wanted as no differences ever arose between the Englands and me but, on the contrary, we were all well content with our adventures, and with each other.

I had visited Stratford-on-Avon several times. My brother John had died while I was yet trying to do something for my living after my Uncle's death, and as I did not hear of my brother's death until after he was buried I made some lines and sent them to my Uncle John, who always loved me, and loved to hear me read and recite things I had of myself composed, even when I was yet a little boy and a scholar at St. Saviours School atte Burslem. None others of my relatives, and not one of my cousins, but laughed at me and derided me: but not so my Uncle John who many a time did take me aside, or did take me away for a ride or a walk, and then asked me to read to him be it the little stories or fables that I had written, or the little poems or odes or songs that I had composed in English—for he knew no Latin or any other tongue but only English.

Also my cousin William had likewise died. He was a wastrel and a vagabond, and a shame and a grief to his father, who oft had said to me— "Would to God that thou wert my son, instead of that drunken, whoring, roystering knave thy cousin, my worthless son."

I bought me a piece of land in Stratford-on-Avon from one Master Edwarde Strattone, a stonemason, for the which I paid him the somme of twenty one pounds, and I built thereon a little house which did cost me more than I had bargained for, for when I settled all the accompts it was more by fifty pounds than I had wished to expend upon it: and I had to borrow the sum of fifty pounds from one Master Edwarde Joyce, haberdasher of Stratford-on-Avon, the which I did pay him back in a year or thereabouts after, with Interest thereon of seven pounds ten shillings, and the costs and charges of his attorney, one Master Miller of Warwicke. I lived in the said house for about a year, for I was very busy with writing a new play, which I finished about the middle of 1590 and I called it

## THE PLAY OF TITUS ANDRONICUS
### A COMEDY BY WILLIAM SHAKSPERE.

I then took it up to London and sold it at once without any difficulty or overmuch huckstering to one Henry Sholton, cousin of the man who had employed me before, and who had derided my first two plays.

He paid me the price for this third play of mine about one hundred and eighteen pounds. It was to be one hundred and twenty pounds, but there were divers deductions for a fresh fair copy, and for his entertainment when he went down to Stratford-on-Avon the when I was awriting it, and hearing parts thereof read to him, and the charges of such journeying that he persisted in reckoning on to the price and deducting the same from the one hundred and twenty pounds—the which I suffered, but not gladly, and forgave him not for doing.

I had some good and dear and trusty friends in London, and made merry with them for nigh to a week together. There were Ben Johnson—a witty and scholarly and a merry rogue, who was very close to my heart, for we two had, years before, been brothers in misfortune, and even want together, and shared our simple lives—and loaves —as well as loves.

And John England, an honest man, and a rare good drinker of ale and mead, and a fine fighter with his fystes.

And Edward England, as honest as John but shy and pale, with a good head for figures, and the best memory in a man that ever I met.

And Edward* Sholton, he who bought my third play, and stopped the money for his journeyings out of the price thereof, but a good roystering companion—at others' charges.

And Will Shakspere, that was I—a small dark

---

* The Sholtons seem intended for the Burbages, but why so designated I do not know. The caprice, or design, or jest, is carried much further with regard to the Christian names, as is apparent throughout.

man with great eyes, whom the women loved not a little but who loved them—not too much; and who was not seldom . . . . called the little Jew boy, or the little Jew from the Midland Counties, which made me to fume with anger: for I knew not then, as I did afterwards, that my grandfather, Thomas the Little of Utrecht in Hollande, had been born a Jew.

I was not a fighter or a drinker of much account, but I was braver than any of them all, and I never knew the inner feeling of the meaning of fear ; and I did holde my owne, and more beside, in any quarrel.

So we five did enjoye ourselves greatly for three days, and went to dance at Sadler's Wells, and to learn to fence at Sheerness in Kent with one Monsieur Darcy, a French Officer who had settled there; and also we went about to Inns, and to Theatres, and to other places not fytte to be here set downe: and I wonder at myself that I do even remember them, for I thought that I had forgotten them like the rains of years ago—long, long times ago.

Then when . . . . . . and bought me some modish clothes and books and other matters,

I went back to Stratford-on-Avon, for already I was bigge with a plan or plotte for a new play.

I begun it on the very morn after my coming home. I had been courting Anne Hathaway, my pretty cousine, and I married her in July 1590 at a church called St. Magdalen and St. Mary in Warwicke, because I was baptised in that saide church, and I also desired my father's blessing, for he was buried in that Churchyard.

I worked harde at my fourth play which I meant to be a monument to my scholarship : for I had been troubled by remarks on my ignorance of the classics and of foreign tongues, forasmuch as my characters had not spoken Latin or French in their parts ; and I was considered an illiterate person, with only a knack at construction of plays because I had, myself, been a player.

I, therefore, designed a play wherein I could show that I also was a person who had learned, and even taught, the humanities; and I broke a fresh ploughshare on a new field, and wrote my place on a page of English History, namely ; *the History of Henry the Fourth.*

I finished that play in July or August 1590 and I called it simply :

## HENRY IV.

### A Tragedy by William Shakspere.

It was in Three Actes and 14 Scenes.

When I had finished it I set to work to fair-copy the same, but that was a weary, long, and tedious labour, in which Anne, my wife, helped me most bravely, for she would reade to me the while I would write, so that, at the end, we were done with it—and done almost to death ourselves also.

I went up to London yet once more with this my fourth play, and with great hopes of speedy wealth and speedy fame.

But, alas! naither came, for none would buy.

All said that I had made a mighty fine play, but all said also that I had made a mighty fine mistake.

It is too long, said one. It is too heavy, quoth another. The subject is not enough entertaining, said the third; and so they went at it, and I was much incensed and could have slain them all.

I had put up at the Inn called the " Plough " in Blackfriars Road, on the other side of the river, and there I met one Master Selard or Stoller or Stellar or some such name—a man of about fifty years of age, and of exceeding gravity, who spake but little but looked wiser than Solon. He was a man from York and had come to London with a scheme for the furthering of legislation for protecting the makers of several kinds of woollen cloths and fabrics. We had much talk together, for I had heard of wool all my life, in Warwicke and in Stratford-on-Avon, and this man's talk did interest me a great deal.

I spoke also to him about my affairs and of my chagrins as to not finding a buyer of my play.

I took him up, one day, into my chamber, and I read to him part of that play ; and he fell to, and spoke to me as if he were the most learned critic in all England, and I the veriest dunce in all Europe.

He called me a waster of honest paper and good quill pens, to say nought of God's gifts of time, and the capacity to work ; and he rated me soundly, and told me to tear the cursed thing to tatters, and go back to my father's trade of wool-dealing, and, maybe, he might help me to do some dyeing, and, perchance, if I feared the Lord, and eschewed ale and the low company of strollers, players, vagabonds, and such like servants of the Devil, I might grow into a grave and stable servant of the Lord.

I did not argue with him, only I said that I would search out the way to keep his worshipful advice in mind and — I did not burn my plays but, contrariwise, I encountered another person —a Master William Shakspere, and that was I myself—and I had a long dialogue with him as thus ;

*I.*—Sir, you do me wrong ; you vex me with your complaints and your persistence and your conceit. I am credibly informed, Sir, that you are a dunce, and a pedant, and a dullard, and a stupid kind of servant of the Devil.

*W.S.*—Sir, you do me wrong most scurvily, for I meant you well. I took you to be a man of wit and some little learning, and I find that you are but a poor and feeble thing, and unworthy of my attention to you, or of the opinion that I was half-willing to entertain about your capacity and judgment.

*I.*—But, Sir, if I be all this, how comes it then that I am not able to sell your play.

*W.S.*—Enough, Sir. The test of a thing is its worth in the scale of sense, and not its weight in the scale of a Grocer.

*I.*—Yet, bethink you, fair Sir ; for if 't be not worth the Grocer's scale how shall you pretend that it has any worth beside ?

*W.S.*—Go, dullard—go to your friend from York, and step out into the dark backyard with him, and strip sheepskins.

*I.*—Now you are angry, and abusive, and do not measure your words as so honourable a man should do. Plainly, Sir, what mean you to do with your play ?

*W.S.*—Sir, I mean to sell it, and to good advantage, too, I warrant you. I shall walk about until I do find a buyer, and if do not——

*I.*—Aye, marry, Sir : and if you do not—what then ?

*W.S.*—Why, then, Sir—Why, then, Sir—why, then I will take a theatre—and play it myself.

*I.*—There spoke my good William Shakspere. Do, Sir—it will be the making of you. Henceforth. try no more to sell it, for I forsee that you shall win much fame and many pounds if you put your resolution to the proof and throw despair out of window.

And thereupon we embraced, and called the drawer to bring us a flagon and a pipe, and we drank success to the play in its new theatre.

I sallied forth next morning and found a house in New Bridge Street, hard by the Bridewell of Blackfriars, and took it on a lease for five years at a rental by the year of one hundred and eighty pounds.   It was a great house, and it cost me over four hundred pounds to alter it and to make it into a good and roomy theatre capable of holding twelve hundred persons at one time .

To raise this huge sum of money I had to engage all the income of the theatre for the first three months, except the wherewithal for to pay the players, and the servants, and the candles, and other charges necessary to be borne for the working of the theatre.

When all was ready this Theatre was opened under the title and name of the

## ROYAL BLACKFRIARS THEATRE

and the piece was my play of HENRY IV.

From the very first night the piece took the populace as well as the Quality, and we overflowed nightly, and could not hold the half of the people who flocked to us, whereat we were rejoiced but, at the same time, we were mournful that so much good money was turned aside and diverted from our exchequer.

Nevertheless, we did mightily well for the space of more than six months, when there was a halt because of some new show that had newly come to London from Italy, with singing men and real women, and not youths as with us.

They performed in The Shire Hall . . . near to the Theatre, and so the people, ever fickle and easily diverted, flocked to The Shire Hall and neglected us ; which seeing I shut up my Theatre, and disbanded my company who were very grieved, and some wept, for they had been well paid and well treated, and the work was easy by reason of the long time that they had played the same piece.

When I came to reckon up and settle all accompts there remained to me the monstrous somme of over one thousand and six hundred pounds : and when I discharged the mortgage charge of Four hundred pounds and the interest thereon I was

left with over twelve hundred pounds clear money
—*and the play was still my own !*

I sold the lease, with all my fittings and fixtures
and utensils and scenes, and all the many things
of all kinds—except the dresses and armour and
arms and ornaments and the like—to one Master
Peter * Sholton, another brother of the man who
had once employed me, for the sum of four hundred
and forty pounds which he paid to me, in part in
money, namely, one hundred and forty pounds,
and in part in bills, namely three hundred pounds,
such bills to become due on equal quarter days
to the intent that each quarter day should see
me paid the sum of twenty five pounds and
interest thereon of ten percentum.

I hastened back to Stratford-on-Avon, where
was my dear wife whom I had not seen for so long,
and she was much rejoiced to see me, and I was
likewise greatly delighted to see her sweet face
again.

In the " first or original cast " were Mr. Prentiss,
Mr. Rentoul, Mr. Sinclaire, Mr. Swinehurst,
Mr. Senelle, Mr. Seeder, Mr. Slow, Mr. Leon, Mr.
Leon 2, Mr. Shakspere, Master Edwardes, Master

* Ante.

Davis, Master Henriques, Master Stephens, Master Davis 3, Master Davis 4, Master Perkins. The rest were soldiers, ladies, lords, etc., etc.

I played both the parts of Hotspur and of Falstaff—albeit my voice was not robust enough for the knight, yet did I monstrously please the people and all who came to see the play.

We performed it twice before the Queen, once at Windsor and once at Greenwich, and her Grace gave us twenty pounds each time, and graciously allowed me for to kiss her hand the which I did gratefully and dutifully.

I stayed at home with my family . . . for some months, and my neighbours made much ado about me and . . . I bought me some houses in the neighbourhood of the Market-place, and a share in the ferry for which I paid one Master Reeves the sum of eighty pounds and four shillings, and I became a man of some weight.

My wife bore me a son, who was born on the sixteenth day of August, 1591, and I was very proud and happy and thought nevermore to have any more concern in plays or players or theatres.

I found that my mother who had married again, and who had died some time before, and who seemed to have lost all thought and affection and care for her children by my father—and we much also for her—had, out of despite, scattered much of the books and papers which my father had cherished, although he had understood but little of them, which had belonged to my grandfather, Thomas the greatly-gifted Jew of Utrecht.

Her second man was a brute and a churl and a drunken hog who had not need to forbid us the house which we, none of us, ever intended to enter.

Now, whether it was really out of despite which, now that I consider the matter I cannot· well think reasonable or probable, or, as is more likely to protect them from her lout and swine of a husband, sure it is that she did make away or hide many of such books and papers, or so many as her husband had left undestroyed. My grief was great when I found that no trace of them could now be found. Those that I had when I was a scholar at St. Saviour's at Burslem were but a handful out of his fine store.

I have said that I thought I should never more have inclination or occasion even to think again about plays or players and theatres.

But I erred mightily. I soon discovered that I had not known myself.

I could not rest quiet and content with my affairs, and my family, and my duties and pleasures, as other men are wont to do.

I could be idle enough, and had no surpassing longing to be for ever hopping and jumping and moving about, and being full of all manners of energies.

On the contrary, I was never happier than I was when doing nothing, or wandering slowly and alone, or sitting tranquilly without noise or speech —or company ; for my own thoughts, and the shapes that my fancy brought forward, were company, and cheer, and food, and exalted happiness to me.

It soon began to irk me that I did not write my thoughts, for many plots and plans of plays had run riot in my brain, and my head was all a-whirl, and often hot and often heavy with no cause to show or plea to make.

I did write many little pieces—lines, songs, sonnets, and the like—the which, much as I have heard my grandfather used for to do, I would mayhap not finish, or leave lying about, or gave away—certes, gave no further heed to.

So, to escape from the seething of my mind, and, perhaps, from the upbraiding of my conscience, I began another play—that is to say, I began to write a play that had for long made a theatre of my mind, and had played to my heart, for the greater part thereof existed already fashioned in my head; and as I walked, or lay abed, and often even as I eat, or listened to my neighbours talking, and seemed to be partaking of their converse, the speeches and the dialogues would go on in my mind, and my imagination would picture forth all the scenes and movements and actions of the piece until oft I knew not whether it were all real, or I were waking, or else dreaming; or, if convinced by touch or other sense that I was really awake, I would almost start affrighted to ask myself, Was I, in truth, quite sane?

My mind was a cauldron. I felt that I had not put its fuels beneath, yet that if they burnt not to their proper use they would of a surety consume me.

I sat down to write and boldly traced the title which was already so familiar to my mind that it

was as if it were like a living child thereof and
not a paper phantom.

## KATHARINA & PETRUCHIO

### OR

## THE TAMING OF THE SHREW.

### BY WILLIAM SHAKSPERE.

———

I had read the merry story in one of my grandfather Thomas his books. It was in English, but
from the Spanish or Portugese—I forget which.

I finished this play in two weeks, and I was not
loth to have a reason to go to London at once.

I had had many letters, and I went this time
with light heart and full of cheer and ease, and
almost indifference to Dame Fortune or her
smiles or frowns.

I have not told that the piece of Katharina and
Petruchio was but as the froth on the tankard and
as the first bloom of the flower of fancy which
was growing so luxuriously in my mind, for I was
filled with far higher matter and far deeper ; and
the writing of this piece was the letting out of the
humours of a full-blooded mind which had else
been almost fevered and freedom-lost.

I had, in fact, already mapped me out my greatest play of

## HAMLET, THE PRINCE OF DENMARK,

almost from the beginning to its ending, with its soliloquies, and dialogues, and all the rest of it ; and I would go afield and declaim, and weep over my declamations, and laugh over my humourous scenes, until all the world besides did seem to disappear and I only, William Shakspere, was left alone in it, wth the creatures of my fancy which had now become my companions and friends and children, and left me and came back to me— not longer at my will and choosing but, the rather, at their own.

So I hailed the going to London with my play of Katharina and Petruchio because it gave me the further diversion, and helped, for the moment, to still the clamourous demands for embodiment and birth of the greater play by giving me occupation and movement, and the stirring about in the active common world of ordinary men and women, and homely doings, and honest getting drunk, or getting sober, and making or losing of moneys, and the like, and the like, and the like.

In London I stayed for the space of a month or so, although my business was done in two days, for Master Sholton made no ado at all about purchasing but at once gave me what I asked therefor, namely : sixty eight pounds. It was seventy pounds, but the Tavern bill when we did sign the Contract brought it down to sixty-eight pounds as I have set forth.

I spent much time with my friend Ben Johnson, and the Englands, and some other choice spirits of my heart, and we made very merry and had trips to France in the brig owned by Master Conwaye. The brig was named " The Syren " of Stephenshythe in Somerset near to the town of Stephensh—I forget the name.

We went to Boulogne where we stayed in a little Inn near the Quay kept by an Englishman named Yeoman or Yeoland, I forget which. He was an old sailor with one leg, and he had the reddest and plumpest nose that I ever beheld in a human face, with a voice like a trumpet in the fog, or like a bellows in the roaring smithy.

We had a merry time . . . and at length we set sail for England in a brig called the " Saucy Nell " whereof one Master Stovel was the Captain, and we reached Rotherhithe once more on the 8th day of July 1593.

Then, because we had all been very sick and ill at ease in our stomachs, we did have a rousing carouse at the King's Head in Eastcheap off Fenchurch Street, and we were all drunk together, and all of us were turned out into the street at twelve of the clock at night and laid by the heels in the Bridewell, which was in the Tower Gate at the end of Eastcheap, where we lay until ten of the clock on the next morning, when I paid the fines of us all to the somme of twelve shillings and fourpence, and we were released and not haled before the Aldermen, whereat I was pleased because of my name—and Ben he did not care one single damn he said, and the Englands seemed as if they were the rather deprived of some renown by a perverse fate in that they were released without any pother or more ceremony than the Get ye gone, ye drunken knaves, from the crusty old warden—to whom I gave a shilling, and Ben a kick in the rump.

Three or four days thereafter I returned me to Stratford-on-Avon.

I hastened almost greedily, because of the time

that I had lost, to see to my affairs and to put what had gathered and tangled and staled into good order ; and forthwith thereafter I put all the world aside, and set me to work.

I remember that I got me to my room and shut fast the door, and I felt as if I had come into some holy chapel out of the outside hurly-burly ; and I cut me six goodly quills, and I kissed them all, one by one, and put them away in a box that I had ; and I gat me paper, and sat me down to write.

I wrote in a great round hand, like as I used to set the lads at Sittingbourne School at Hoddingley where I was once an Under-Usher—

## HAMLET, PRINCE OF DENMARK.

### A TRAGEDY BY
### WILLIAM SHAKESPERE.

But when I wanted to begin to write, after I had written the Dramatis Personæ, and the heading of Scene I. Act 1, not a word would there come to my mind or to my liking.

But, instead, whole scenes would rise and act themselves, and pass in pomp, or in horror, or in laughter, or in awe ; and Laertes would stab

Hamlet, and Hamlet would stab Polonius, and Ophelia would come to the Queen, and the Grave-digger would talk to Horatio, and the King and the Ghost would have a talk together in the green-room, and all the rest would be ranting, each in his own way, and at times all of them together, in my hot head and fantasy.

I could not calm my mind, for it was too full, and the play had been, in nearly all its parts, too well composed, for me to begin writing it down as if it were all fresh and virgin, save only the idea or plot and the bare outline. I was encumbered, and well-nigh overwhelmed, with the weight of my own too complete work of preparation.

At length, however, I settled myself down and began.

How I laboured!

I took no thought for rest, or food, or exercise ; but sometimes I would steal away and go out into the woods, speaking to none and answering no man not even his kindly salutation, for I scarce knew if he or I were real, or if my eye brought me the true intelligence or my surroundings. And there would I sit, and ramble, and look up, and wring my hands, or, as the case might call for it, laugh and speak in diverse voices, and fence, and fall, and strut, and lay about, and set up my travelling booth, and otherwise make of the trees and shades theatres and castles and ramparts and palaces, and I—faith! I was everybody by turns —even though I had to be like two or more at the same time.

It was passing strange—and it at times made me to think that our souls were greater by far than ever we imagined or could conceive—that, quick as were these changes in my fancied impersonations, I yet felt afresh in every one of them as if I had been the real, and not that imagined one ; born and bred and living and aching with him and her in the innermost springs and founts of original being and separate mortal form.

I said once, methinks, that my mind was a cauldron.

But now it was as a furnace.

The rather was it as a potter's oven—but a potter's oven which in some mysterious or fantastic manner had fellowship and keenest sympathy with every pot and image and shard that was baking within it.

I loved best of all Hamlet's soliloquoy " To be or not To be," and also his talk with the Ghost, and his behaviour when he watched the King and Queen, his mother, at the scene of the players.

I think that I had seen some writing of my grandfather Thomas—an Essay on Immortality, if I remember rightly—in which there were some of the passages which I used in that soliloquoy. It was an unfinished piece, and had slipped into a book which I had with me when I was a scholar at St. Saviour's School, Burslem. I am sorry that I have mislaid that book. It was in French. It was called La Chose essentielle aux Hommes . . . —I may remember later, but 'tis no matter.

Thus did I labour and not spare myself, nor candles either, until all was done and I could ring down the curtain on the very end—and that was on the 2nd day of December 1593.

I remember well that day for I went and tore up all my foul sheets of paper, and burnt all my broken but faithful quills, and I went and kissed my wife and child, and every woman and girl in the house, and I called for a full flagon of wine which I drank to the very dregs, and then I danced by myself in the middle of the kitchen, to the amazement of my wife and the maids : and then I went out and gathered several of my good friends and neighbours, and we went and had a rousing carouse at the Neptune Inn in Stratford-on-Avon, which was then kept by one Master Selery or Sillery, I mind not which.

A few days thereafter I set out for London yet once again, and I put up at the Inn called the Three Swans in Bishopsgate, and there came to see me Ben Johnson, who had become fat and rather careless and dirty, but a rare good fellow and a ripe scholar ; and the Englands, and both the Sholtons and others of my acquaintance—to the whom I had sent letters to inform them of my coming.

It was not long before I found a buyer of this my greatest play as yet, and which I never thought that I could excel—no, nor could any man now living, as I used to say to my own conceit. Yet it was true : for so I felt in my most secret mind, and so was I ready almost to praise the writer thereof as if it had been some other than myself.

Nay, and I often afterwards marvelled at parts thereof when I did read them, and hard work to persuade myself that I did indeed write them; and I had so persuaded myself of the verity I then marvelled the more, for it seemed as if it was some other writing by my mind and by my hand—leaving me to read or hear and wonder as if I were one of the populace who had paid his eightpence to see the piece from the rear of the theatre.

I got the great somme of *one thousand* pounds for that *great* play.

It was Master Sholton in company with Master Bowen and likewise with Master Stevens who bought it.

I agreed to stay in London for six months so that I might help instruct the players and to supervise the preparations for the coming out of the play at the Royal Blackfriars Theatre, whereof Master Sholton was the Owner.

I did faithfully my duty, and selected and instructed all the players, and I agreed to play therein myself at first, so that by my presence I might help and keep all in mind of their instructions.

The first performance was on the 2nd of July 1594. It was thus announced—

ROYAL BLACKFRIARS THEATRE.

On the 2nd July, 1594,

HER GRACES SERVANTS

Will perform the

TRAGEDY

of

HAMLET, PRINCE OF DENMARK,

by

WILLIAM SHAKESPERE.

This Tragedy is founded on the Scandinavian story of Hamlet, and has been composed and invented in 3 Actes and 11 Scenes by the Queen's most humble servant William Shakespere.

The Doores will be opened by Six o'clock, and the performance will begin at half past six of the clock.

There will be a rest of ten minutes between the Actes 2 and 3, and those wishing to go out may do so and enter again upon a cheque or pass to be granted to them on going out.

The prices are as follows, namely :—
The Boxes are of the price of One Guinea the Box.
The Pit is of the price of One shilling each person.
The Gallery is of the price of Sixpence each person.
Those at the rear of the Pit shall pay only Eightpence but cannot have any seat to sit down in.

The Music will play at times.

GOD SAVE THE QUEEN.

This Bill was on a board outside the theatre, and was written out fresh every day. There were many poor scholars who did make copies thereof and disposed of the same at their own risk and for their own profits at the doors, or in the coffee houses ; and some got a penny or two, and some got sixpence or more for the same.

The manner of advertising was as follows :—

The bellman would go round—each in his Parish—and publish the coming out of the play, and there would be advertisements in the Gazette and in other Journals, and copies of the bills would be put in the windows of coffee-houses and on walls and elsewhere. These were printed and of the size of a big man's hand. Also the players would go round to the houses of the Quality, and to the shops and offices of merchants, and to the Temple and Inns of Court, and to the officers of the Army and the Navy, and to the Inns where Travellers did stay, and I know not what more or what other places and persons, and solicit patronage and dispose of tickets on which they were allowed a poundage of so much, generally one shilling in the pound, which they were very glad to earn.

It did often happen, however, that players

would be made so drunk while going about in the daytime that they were sorely put to it to do their parts at night. In such case they were fined, but their comrades mostly stood bravely by them and pulled them through—and the pump in the yard did ungrudgingly do its share in the succour.

The first Cast of Hamlet was as follows :—

| | | |
|---|---|---|
| Hamlet by .. .. .. | | Mr. Prentiss. |
| Horatio .. .. .. | | Mr. Peake. |
| The King .. .. | | Mr. Stevens. |
| The Ghost.. .. | | Mr. Shakspere. |
| Polonius .. .. | | Mr. Sheptone. |
| Laertes .. .. | | Mr. Melton. |
| Gravedigger .. .. | | |
| Ditto 2 .. .. | | |
| Rosencrantz .. .. | | |
| Gildenberg .. .. | | |
| First Player .. .. | | |
| Second ,, .. .. | | |
| The Queen .. .. | | Master Stevens 5. |
| Ophelia .. .. .. | | Master Stevens 6. |
| Amelia .. .. .. | | Master Stevens 7. |

Soldiers, Courtiers, Ladies, etc., etc., etc.

(Those marked Stevens, 2, 3, 4, 5, 6, 7, were the parts supplied by him. I forget the names, but I do remember that he had to supply, the which he did, so I indicate them by his name and a No.)

The players were paid thus—

Hamlet had for his pay the somme of 33/- by the week.

| | | | |
|---|---|---|---|
| Horatio | ,, | 21/6 | ,, |
| The King | ,, | 21/6 | ,, |
| The Ghost | ,, | 21/6 | ,, |
| Polonius | ,, | 30/6 | ., |
| Laertes | ,, | 20/6 | ,, |
| Gravedigger | ,, | 15/6 | ,, |
| ,, 2 | ,, | 8/6 | ,, |
| Rosencrantz | ,, | 8/6 | ,, |
| Gilderstern | ,, | 8/6 | ,, |
| The Queen | ,, | 8/6 | ,, |
| Ophelia | ,, | 8/6 | ,, |

Soldiers, Courtiers, Ladies, etc., each 4/6 by the week or 9 pence for the night every night when paid nightly, as was sometimes done for their convenience, as they were chiefly very poor men —disbanded soldiers, and the like—and could not live until the week were ended without their daily or nightly money.

The Music was thus :

| | | |
|---|---|---|
| One Hautboy | ........8/6 | by the week. |
| One Flute | .........8/6 | ,, |
| One Fife | .........8/6 | ,, |
| One Cymbal | ........8/6 | ,, |
| One Drum | .........8/6 | ,, |

And the Master of the Music he did likewise play some instrument as suited the occasion—such as another flute, or a viol, or a trumpet—and he was paid :

The Master of the Music 8/6 by the day which was by the week 51/-.

He was one Signor Emilio Solenni or Sollone, I mind me not the which, but it matters not.

We had also the money-takers, of whom there were four—two for the Pit and Boxes, and two for the Gallery—and we paid them :

Four Money-takers, each man of them 8/6 by the week.

and also Four Ticket-takers each man of them 8/6 by the week,

and Eight Candlemen and Snuffers, each man of them, 8/6 by the week,

and Six men for to keep the populace in order with their staves, and to eject those who were unruly or drunk, or who made too loud noises by shouting or swearing or whistleing, or otherwise misbehanved to the hindrance of the players or to the discomfort or angering of the assembly—each man of them—8/6 by the week.

And there were the Sweepers and Cleaners—a

dozen or more of sturdy women—each woman sixpence by the day, and two pints of small-ale and some bread and cheese.

I was the Manager of the Stage, and I did receive for that work about six pounds at the settling up of all the matters at the end.

There was likewise a Prompter who did receive 20/6 by the week.

The Scriveners who did copy out the several parts were paid two pennies for every one hundred and sixty words.

The candles consumed on every night were about eighty pounds, and they did cost not less than eight pounds—that is, two shillings for each pound, for that they were fat and big and burned slow and bright. They were not of tallow, but of pure Italian wax, and they were made by one Master Gunning of the Mall, near to Charing Cross, where he had a shoppe ; but his factory was at London Fields because of the foul smells, for he did make tallow candles also in great quantity.

We reckoned thus—

OUR OUTGOINGS OF EVERY SORT by the week
£85 10 0
OUR INCOMINGS        ,,        ,,        £150 0 0

We had also to add to the outgoings the Rent of the Theatre ; and the Queen's share of the incomings, which was one shilling in every one pound ; and also the cost of repairs, and the Impositions of the Ward, and others the like ; and of the waste and disrepair of the scenery and of the dresses, and so forth ; the all which being taken into accompt, and reckoned in, would swell the Outgoings to wellnigh Ninety pounds by the week.*

We paid for the painting and making of all the scenes, and for all the stuff in them, to one Master John Dibden or Dibben the sum of twelve pounds 10/--.

And we paid to one Master Edwarde Shankes, and to one Mistress Shanks—but not in business together with Edward—altogether the sum of over thirty two pounds for dresses and cloaks and hose and robes and other apparel for all the players, and eke the helpers in the play.

I did not ask or receive anything whatsoever from the performing of the play except my wages, and the allowance at the end for the general superintendence of the stage, and the parts, and

* The sum total seems understated.

the rest of it ; for I had sold it totem quotem and had no further rights thereto.

Master Prentiss was a fine player ; and he did play the part and spoke the soliloquies in such a way that I, who listened to him and observed him from the wings, had all my work to do to keep me from running on the stage and clasping him in my arms in the sight of all the people in the theatre.

My heart leaped within my bosom as I heard him declaim, and stop, and recommence, and pause again, and go vehemently on, or, as half-despairing, sigh with the meaning and the burden of my words.

I needed to remind myself that they were mine, and not another man's—and yet it seemed to me that they were so far above me, and of my daily life and occupations, and companionships, and low and worldly manner of going and speaking and doing—that it could not be—it could not be—as I said passionately to myself : and all but accused myself of a dishonest thing and act in that I had put it all forward as my work, and had got money therefor, and had seen it, an hour or less before, on the playbill at the door, with my name written thereon as the Author.

I thought I was an imposter. But no—the

bitter reminder came, and I remembered all the
pains and joys of the childbirth, and I thanked
God that there was that Other of me—that other
concealed William Shakspere who did, at times,
visit Me, his common and outward representative
and agent and alter ego: and, enforcing the service
of my organs—my eyes and hands—did indite
these glorious thoughts, and then withdraw himself again, I know not whither—but leaving me
with some few rakings of his fires for to do such
minot things unworthy of that Other, as Katharine
and Petruchio, and the like.

And sometimes—for at times I was much alone
as I loved to be, and would have none of company
or even of books—it pleased me to think of that
Other, and to wonder whether it had fallen to me
alone to be thus Double ; but sometimes it would
take me to dream, with open eye and roaming
fancy, whether that nobler, higher, greater Other
was not a part of my real singular self; and most
likely—for nothing else in all the world so well
fitted into my thought, and even into all the facts
and circumstances—my grandfather Thomas of
Utrecht visited me, and used me for his secretary
—and glorified me in the using.

I have never before spoken of this to any man, or trusted it to any paper ; and I had almost the remembrance of the angers and shames which I felt when the ladies had called me the pretty Jew boy, and when, as I grew older, others called me in derision the little Jew ; and how I was hotly furious at being thus miscalled. But after the writing of this my play of Hamlet, and especially after I had seen it played nightly, and the great-ness thereof being more and more manifest—and the littleness and commonness of me likewise more apparent, and, by the contrast, even more frequently light and unworthy and earthly and of low degree—*

Ever after this time, whenever I did write any-thing of a lofty nature, or anything of a lightsome poetic strain, or was surprised into, or rather by, a happy turn of thought, or phrase, or of com-parison, or any broidery of imagination, or any sublimity of diction, I always pictured to myself that magnificent and self-and-world-neglected little genius, Thomas the Jew of Utrecht ; who had been borne by a thousand chances and mis-chances to be the progenitor and Master and owner

* This sentence *seems* involved, but it is only incomplete.

and honoured Guest and Visitor of one most unworthy of that supreme honour [yet not unworthy
inasmuch as he did perceive it was an honour,
and himself strove to be no idle or dull (at great
degree) disciple and fond imitator] William
Shakspere of Stratford-on-Avon, who had received
*one thousand pounds for the play of Hamlet,* and
who was acclaimed by all the town as the rarest
dramatical poet of the day.

And, in truth, so they did.

The Queen did order the play to be played before
her five times in all, twice at Windsor, once at
Greenwich, once at Stevenage and once at—
plague on't !—at—nay,—but I will have it, you
jade of a Memory, and be damned to you for a
despicable b . . . of a stealthy Ale-wife's cat !
—and once at the George's Head in Eastcheap—
no, the Glover's Hall in Eastcheap, when they did
one day feast her Grace, and all her Courtiers,
and Ladies, and High commanders, and Councillors.

She paid for each performance thirty one pounds
and ten shillings ; and the Worshipful Company
of Glovers did pay for that performance in their
Hall forty two pounds, and did besides right
royally entertain all the players, and, notably,

myself, who was allowed by the Queen for to kiss her hand, the which I gratefully and dutifully did ; and the Worshipful Master of that worthy and Ancient Guild did pledge a glass to me, William Shakspere, for that I was the author of that great play, as he called the same ; and all the company cried Hurrah many times, and all the ladies did clap their hands.

I spoke a piece in thankfullness of the big honour which they had done a humble writer and servant of the Queen, and when I sat down the Worshipful master he sent me a gold cup and said it was to be a gift from himself and the Guild to me, and to be with me and my children from henceforth and evermore.

And I was thankful when that her Grace rose to go away, and the merry company broke up, and we of the players' company did pack up and take us to our carts and waggons to go back to Black-friars ; for the burden of the praises and honours was like to have [made] me shout like a mad thing, or else swoon like a weak woman.

Yet, ever as men spoke, and cheered with right good heart, and fair women smiled and cried sweet vivats, and waved their kerchiefs or scarves, or their white arms, and their eyes shining in their rosy faces, and their gleaming teeth enhancing their ruby lips, I seemed to see the shape—as my fancy presented him, for I never saw any presentment of him—of my grandfather, Thomas of Utrecht; and I almost took myself by the collar, and shook myself like a malefactor is shaken when he is caught in flagrante delicto, for that I was taking all the honours, whereas I was but as the scribe, and he, Thomas the Jew of Utrecht, the real and rightful heir of all these plaudits and high compliments and commendations.

Belike, I was a big foole; and, belike, I was in an overworked and overstrained mind and nerve; and, belike, it was that I was looking at my work which I had done in one high temperature of mind and soul and fancy while I was in a very different degree and character of the same; and, belike, it was a silly fancy or an overwrought phantasm, if I may so express it.   But I felt it no disparagement to myself to make so much attribution to him: nay, and the more I might be right in doing this the greater indeed my glory and distinguished grace, forasmuch as it would then be sooth that he had stooped from his starry splendour wherein

I never doubted that he dwelt, to work and inspire, and fnake use of me, his humble scion, who, with his blood, had likewise inherited some little of his fervour, and tracery, and unfathomed depths of soul, and unceasing questioning, and unspoken longings, and peeps at times into the sounding vestibules of the Eternal halls ; and—as roll the rivers from unknown sources and majestically sweep by to their deep bournes—the words seemed to come unbidden in wave on wave and billow on billow, till that the eye grew giddy and the hand faint and stiff in that it could not as swiftly record them.

I am lost in the light of his light, and I was but as the shadow thrown by him. Nevertheless, I was not forgetful of myself, inasmuch as I believed myself to be the direct inheritor and mirror of his genius, and honoured by his selecting of me out of all the men upon this earth.

And yet it sometimes seemed to me as if my soul was playing hide-and-seek with itself, and that my adoration of my gifted ancestor was but a secret sophistication of my own mind to conceal the vast and inexpressible vanities and exaltations which I felt because I had written *Hamlet*, and because I admired it, myself, a thousand times more than they all who did shout thereat, and clap their hands and stamp with their feet and cry out hurrahs when I came into a coffee-house, or was recognised in the street—for so great had become my fame.

Thus shall a man play at games with himself, as if he were playing a part to other men, and, as jugglers do—toss up balls into the air, and catch them again, and hide some and extract others from where they had not been supposed to be, and pretend to place others where he doth put them not, but all to deceive the eye and the mind of the looker on—so did I.   Else my love and most high opinion of my own work had been disrobed, and I left abashed at the very effrontery of my vanity, or made ridiculous as was Narcissus who became enamoured of his own reflection, and died thereof— and a good riddance for a most egregious coxcomb and fool.

When I got me back to my house at Stratford-on-Avon the whole town rose up to welcome me, and the Warden and Burgesses, and all the men and women and children and dogs of the town did come forth to greet me, as I was entering the town by the London Road, in my own wagon, which I had bought for mine own use to journey to my home, of one Master Hewett of Bartholemy's Lane for the somme of twenty two pounds and eight shillings, for the which great somme I did get—imprimis : A very good and strong wagon with iron rims on the wheels thereof.

Two strong but eke rough horses, aged the one seven years, and the other about nine years, strong but slow—but that did not matter one damn to me because that I was not in any hurry, and because I was never comfortable in any coach or chariot that went too quickly.

Very good harness of leather, and much brass thereon, and little bells of which there were many.

Very good covering for the wagon, and cloths for the horses, and nosebags for the same, and two whippes.

Sundrie smaller matters and implements, all very useful but not necessary to set down in detail of the same.

I had bought in London many things for my wife, and for my child, and for a score or more relations and dear friends, such as

Two gowns of silke from Master Simpkens of the Cheapside shoppe.

One mantle of the same, but made in the French mode, with many cuttings and slashings and trimmings and the Ebony God knows what.

Great store of linen for her wear, and for her use for bed and other services, and ribbons, and scissors, and small-ware, and French trifles—Oh, I would as lief pay for them all again rather than have to enumerate them.

Stores of sweetmeats and confections from France, and long golden chains for her neck, and baubles for the child, and trinkets and gauds, and a very miscellany of rare and pretty things, and strange spices, and some curiously wrought pipes and pouches for the holding of tobacco, and the like, and the like, and the like, beyond all remembering or setting forth.

Also there were clothes for myself, and many bookes, many bookes, every one of them a treasure and a delight to me.

I took with me for my company, and likewise for my protection, two sturdy knaves ; and also my good friend Edmund* England who was a

* Obviously intended for Edward.

brave and courageous man and could shoote well
with gun or with crossbow ; and there was also
the teamster and his boy—the which boy was a
man of bigger build than himself—who could' eat
what would surfeit two ploughmen and a dog
besides, and he could drink what would be nigh
to the drowning of the three of them.

For on a day when we were on the road, and were
laying at Enfield, I think—or maybe it was at
Elmhurst, or perchance Elmanhurst—I do forget
which, but I shall remember on the revising hereof
—Master England he took it into his merry stupide
head to prove by mathematical measurement,
and the endroit and the mensuration tables,
how much ale that saide boy could drink before
he would become drunken, or fall asleep, or become
furious, or, what seemed much harder to conceive of, gay and dancing mirthful.

He laid me a wager of four shillings that he
would drink about eight quarts, which is two
gallons, and I lay the wager, and we did put the
eight shillings, the one atop of the other, and placed
the silver column in a cup and put it on one side for
the winner of the wager. The " boy "—methinks
his name was John —— some name like Luck or

Lack or Lank or the like—was not at all loth to try, and although I knew full well that he could drink a monstrous deal, yet it seemed to me that he could not swill down two gallons ; for I knew besides that he had been already drinking divers quarts, and Edwarde he had not bargained that John should begin on a fasting or ale-less stomach —and I did not remind him to bargain for it.

John made no ado, when the horses were put up for the night at the Inn where we did lay, but he called for his supper and he began his potations as if it [were] his mother's milk.

Lord ! How the quarts melted down his fiery satietyless throat ! It was not forbidden by the laws of the wager that he should be limited by us, or either of us, in his eatinge, for whereas Edmonde was of the mind that more eating would help his drinking I was of the mind that as human and anatomical capacity was not unbounded it would shorten his drinking.

John was a good man of his teeth also, and he eat the further viands which the landlord brought him at our bidding—bread and cold meat and a capon, or the greater part thereof, and a dish of minced meats the which was hot, and cheese, and other items of one sort and another. John was not a man of witte nor of many words, and if he had any thoughts no one ever knew them, and belike they were unknown to himself, and of fancy he had as much high esteem as a cartwheel has of melody. Yet his dull and most fish-like eye did for an instant sparkle, as doth a puddle at a passing lanthorn, when the meats were placed within his reach and at his mercy.

The emptied alepots stood in a stately row and told the tale of his progress and the fortunes of the wagerers, and my heart began to misgive me, for he was becoming the more ravenous and sober the more he eat and drank, and I feared me greatly for my four shillings, and eke the charges of his so great eatinge and drinkinge—the which were to be borne by the wagerer who lost the wager.

The other knaves did mightily envy John his happy and unstinted lot, and they, and likewise many others in the Inn, did also make their own petty wagers on the event or outcome of the pleasantry.

But my fortitude did forsake me altogether when the insatiable and silent John, who had diligently applied himself unto his gourmandise

without so much as a word or a grin to anybody,
did of a sudden open that dread mouth of his for a
purpose other than to thrust therein solid foods
or to pour therein liquid refreshmentings—it
was when he had finished seven fearful quarts—
and to break into speech for the first time during
the performance, for I warrant me the villain had
not said a grace—not even in a whisper.

Quoth he, the while we all started to hear him—

Good Masters, who will wager with me, on the
foot of four shillings for every shilling of mine,
that I shall not drink four quarts the more beyond
these eight—at the charges of the loser of the
wager—and then walk by myself to my straw in
the stable for my sleep ?

And while some were astonished, and some
thought him a braggart, and some winked and
smiled and thought that the ale had taken holde of
his brain, I quickly perceived me of his prowess in
the matter of the drinkinge of ale, and I keenly
observed that he was not without himself, but
valiant and capable, and blood-cold, and un-
scathed by the quantities that he had taken; and I
was minded to have my sport, and my laugh, and
my money back, or like to lose a little more—

and what odds for that! The sport was a right merry one.

So I cried—

Knave, I cannot wager with thee, nor take thy money if thou shouldst lose thy wager. Yet will I, for the good sport of it, wager with any one here not being of my service, and I will wager it once— my shilling to every three, and not four, of any others ; and I will wager it again, and yet a third time, and still again with a fourth man, and a fifth man ; and here be my five shillings, or as many of them as shall back my challenge if any here do answer it ; and I shall give thee, John, if I shall win, one whole shilling out of every separate wager that I do draw the wagered money for.

I will wager, and I, and I, and I, and I, cried one, and another, and many : but I was content with five of the seemliest and gravest men who were there ; and all the money—twenty shillings —was counted and gathered into the custody and keeping of the landlord to abide the end. Other wagers were made amongst themselves by others, but these concerned me not.

There was dispute and argument whether John

should be allowed to have his head under the pump for a space, or to have a rest and a pipe of tobacco, or anyway to take the air for a little while outside the door ; but John cut short all the talk and clamour in a speech whereof the brevity was most admirable and the pith thereof most pellucid clear.

Saith John—Not a damn care I. Bring in the ale, and eke some bread and cheese. It were a merry tale to tell, were it not for its length, and 'twas too rich and rare to be circumscribed or curtailed, but the undaunted and unslaked John did easily accomplish his dozen quarts, and drank a brimming cup of mulled sack which I did give him at the end, with the five shillings which I had promised him, for to warm his drowned and deluged stomach ; and he did but once wax eloquent with a wink of his eye, and walked without a stumble or a hiccup to his straw in the stable.

Edmunde had given him two shillings also, and I was not, or scarce, the loser, for the fine sport and entertainment and marvellous experiment, when all was settled with the landlord at the next morning.

I had a troubled conscience in the night and feared and fancied that the valorous John might die of an apoplexy in his straw, for no man, I thought, had minded him to undo a button of his raiment, and he might die of an apoplexy or be choked or strangled in some helpless way.

So I stole me down out of my bed with a lanthorn to look at him, and he was sleeping like a blessed child that had the trick of snorting between its dimpled smilings. I turned him gently on his side, and left him well contented.

I did not carry my Thousand pounds in my wagon, nor had it hidden in my lodgings. On the very day that I did receive it, and almost within the hour, I paid it to my credit to the Bankers to Her Grace, the Brothers Silver and Company of Cornhill, who were Goldsmiths and silversmiths and banking men, and who allowed me interest thereon at 8 percentum, and I could retire my money, or any part thereof, on notice to them of one month wherever I might be residing in England or in any part of Europe.

I was, therefore, easy upon that score, for I ween that prudence in the keeping is often more difficult than is skill in the getting.

It must not be thought that because I did at times sit, as it were, with ungartered hose, and had my easy laugh and my lazy yawn, that therefore I was forgetting that I was less than I was or more than I seemed, or that I would not, when the silent call for worthy work should come, be ready to caparizon myself thereto in other guise and company.

I hold it ill of any to suppose that I was a man of low habit or life, for it is the contrary that is true. I abhorred utterly all low, vulgar, and mean things ; but I hold it also true that to be of a frolicsome nature at times, after great strain and stress, is of a most useful and wholesome blessing, and debases not the mind that is undebased, but relaxes the too long tension of the bowstrings of life.

I might sing—

> Hand me up my trusty bow,
> And hand me too my sword,
> For I will go to war no more,
> Nor wait upon my lord.
>
> My lord is gone to woo and wed,
> And my lord is gone from me,
> And I see not why I should trouble me
> For quarrels are not for me.

For me, instead, the homely nook,
The good wife's smile and eye,
The ale-pot and the cheery pipe,
And let the world go by.

For quarrels are the devil's game,
And wars the play of fools,
And honest men were never made
To be the Nobles' tools.

And I am sick of wars and din,
And oaths and shouts and blare ;
A little cot and loving wife
My tranquil lot to share !

So sing ho ! to love and ale and peace,
And down with battles all !
And he's a knave who will not drink
This toast with heart and call.
    Sing Ho ! Sing Hey ! Sing Ho ! and Ho !
    and Ho !

This is an old song, but I have forgotten much,
and substituted words, etc., where I had forgotten.

After this I rested awhile, and looked after my
affairs, and bought me some parcels of land and
houses, and a share in the ferry, and also a share
in the Shop of one Thomas Glover, a maker of
ploughs and other smithwork, unto whom I paid
the sum of one Hundred and twenty pounds for

one fourth share or part of all his earnings for the space of five years, the which proved an unprofitable business, for he went and drank for a full month, at the end whereof the bailiff seized his smithy and all that was therein, and he was made bankrupt and put into Stamford gaol where he lay for wellnigh three years.

But I was soon tired of all this tranquil world of petty life, and my great relief and joy was to escape from it all to my beloved quills and quires of paper.

I had more than one plot or plan for plays all prepared, and ere long I was at it ding-dong with all my might.

I began as I always did with the title of my play thus—

## HENRY THE Vth.

### A TRAGEDY IN FIVE ACTS.

#### BY

#### WILLIAM SHAKSPERE.

I laboured upon this historical play for over eight months, working often more than sixteen hours of the day. I refused to see visitors, and would not write letters, or go to any of the numerous meetings and merry-makings and markets and

other assemblages ; or even to quit my house
except to go of an evening, and quite alone, for a
ramble in the woods for my health's sake, to take
the stiffness from my legs and the crookedness
from my back.

I used to go to a particular spot near where the
Avon bends and loops and turns and shows its
shallows and shinglings by the side of the big
tree that hangs over a steep bank near East
Redeham, close to the place where once stood a
post to mark the way to the village.

There would I roam, and sit, and walk, and
declaime my great speeches of Hotspur and Wolsey
and Prince Henry and my merry Knight Sir
John and his frisky knaves, Pistol and Bardolph,
and Shelford and Stamford and Katherine, and
Dame Quickly and Doll Tearsheet and the rest.*

Most chiefly did I love the parts where the
Knight did try to impose upon Prince Hal, and
also where the Cardinal fell and lamented his fall.

I remember one day, as I walked and declaimed
in loud tones—thinking I was all alone, and
unheard and unseen—the lines

* It will be seen that there is much confusion of memory in this
and in the following paragraph. These are but instances.

Oh Cromwell, Cromwell, had I but served my God
With half the zeal I served my King He would not
Now have left me desolate.

A voice answered me from among the briar.

" Hey, Master, be not so downhearted ; there's
many a cheery day left for thee : be thou but
bold and put a good face on t' matter."

I turned me quickly with burning face, and
found a burly honest fellow, leg-weary, ragged,
but jovial, although he possessed not a penny, or a
button to his jerkin which was mended and held
together by bits of string.

Quoth I to him when I had surveyed him
enough, which took not long—" Honest man,"
quoth I, " who art thou and what is thy condition,
and wherefore art thou in this plight ? "

"I!" laughed he, merrily—" I am well eno',
for I have eaten once today, and I can sleep
beneath a bush, and tomorrow—if God will—I
shall eat again, and if not, I shall go a-hungred ;
but I shall not be sad, no, nor over sorry, for why ?
I'm a man—and this is the world, and yon's the
sun, and beyond is—God ; and if he doesn't look
after his own works he is a carelesser master than
I take him for."

And with that he gathered himself, and shook with laughter, and trolled a song :

> For he is but half a man who cries
> When the billow goes too strong ;
> Better he who bravely tries,
> To swim and get along.
> And he [who] falls away and sighs,
> Is but a craven and a fool—
> For only once a man he dies,
> And here's my sermon, and my school.
> Tra la, la, la, la.

"Thou art a merry knave," I said to him, admiring his care-free fashion of thinking and living, "and prithee, how dost thou in the winter ?"

"Why, Master," said he, "in the Winter I just go and live in a hut in the woods, and I kill rabbits and hares, and snare birds, and eke fish, and cadge bread and salt, and mayhap sell some skins and birds or poles or withes, and buy me ale or shoes, or flints for my firings, and bowstrings, and whatnot ; and 'tis a jolly life and a happy one, and I do not envy the King Henry thou wert shouting for, my master ; no, nor any other son of a man in all merry England—damned if I do !"

I marvelled at his bold spirit, and methought there was that below the skin and manner of the man which might be worth the while to learn. So I said to him—

"My honest friend," I said, "I am not in any distress or trouble. I was but repeating something that I had read which pleased me hugely; but thou, meseems, would be the better for a full meal, and a suit of leather, and some shillings in thy pouch for a rainy day—and this shalt thou have from me, and welcome; but tell me first, good fellow, whence thou camest here—for thy speech is none of these parts—and why thou hast chosen to waste thy life in this manner, for thou art strong of body, and as I do perceive myself, not so rude and unlearned of mind as thy appearance and seeming go to tell. Speak to me openly as to a friend,"—I added this for I saw a shade as of a sudden pain shoot atwhart his sunburnt face.

He paused a goodly while, and questioned my face long with his eyes. Twice he seemed as if about to speak and twice he did stop. At length, said he, in a voice so strangely changed that I started as I stood there before him:

"Sir," said he, and the very texture and inflexion of his tone fell like another man's on my astonished ears—" I am not what I seem, and I seem what I am not. I am a gentleman, and I take you also for a scholar and a gentle sir. Therefore do I speak so plain and hold up my secret to your gaze, for well know I that you are too noble to betray it."

I said in answer :

" My good and gentle sir : I am too truly a friend to all good men in any strait or distress for to break their faith in me, or for me to break my honour to them."

" Sir, I thank you with all my heart," said he. " If you will sit down on this prostrate tree I will lean against its standing cousin here opposite, and in brief terms inform you wherefore I am thus, and live an hermit's and a vagabond's life in these woods.

" I am the Lord of . . . and I was a happy and contented squire till I did let my brother come and dwell with me.

" He—but 'twere tedious to tell you all the tale —he brought me to my ruin, for he swore I was a complice in a league against our Queen—and when I fled, until that I could bring proof to right myself, he seized my goods, and got my wife to bed with him, and sent my children to a distant house of mine, and stole my moneys and my name, and my good title to all honest men's regard, by his lies and damned villany.

"A faithful swain brought me word, in my secret hiding-place, that I had been outlawed— and, sir, here I am.

"But not all that fate has wrought me shall subdue my spirit. I am like Prometheus bound to his rock, and his vitals pecked at by the hungry beaks of birds of prey, and all the torments that can torture soul and body let loose upon me.

"But I do feel within me a sustaining power, and I do hear within my soul an upholding voice, and I am like Job, who held fast his own integrity and knew that the great God of all still lived, and saw, and suffered to be done, all that had happened —and kept the just accompt thereof.

"Therefore I repined not, nor complained, but resolved for to bear and to endure—and this, gentle sir, is all my tale. And so God save you, sir, for I go on my way to see how fares my rabbit snare."

"Nay, nay, good Sir," I cried, "we part not so.

Your hand, my unsoured Diogenes—my noble, patient, and Heaven-trusting friend. In turn, I speak the word of cheer to you. An end will come to all this monstrous wrong, and your light shall shine again. As to your jade of a wife, let the b—— go hang! She is no more wife of thine, and the devil, and any of his helots' helots, may have her. Set thou never eyes on her again nor think of her—a score like her were not worth one minute's thought of a man like thou. And as for thy present state and needs, I will take thee at my charge from this day forth."

"Sir, I do thank you most fervently," he answered, with a bow and a trembling lip, "but I cannot endanger you, for I am an outlaw. Yet this will I accept at your gracious hand—a crown, a leathern suit, a pair of shoon, a knife and a hatchet—and entire oblivion of me as if we had never met, or, meeting, had for ever forsworn our acquaintance, and resolved to meet not again."

We had further talk, and after our farewell he turned and in an instant, as if he had been an apparition, he disappeared into the woods, without the crackling of a twig or the disturbance of a bush or bough.

I brought all the things he had named—and some others besides that he had not stated in his inventories—on the next day, and having, as we had agreed, made our signs the one to the other, I walked away; and when, within the half hour, I passed that spot again all had gone, and not a sign remained of them or of him. I never saw him again.

It came to my knowledge some later time that he had regained all his honours and possessions—except of his false and polluted wife, who did most righteously execute herself by leaping headlong from a high tower in the dwelling she had so pestilently dishonoured. His traitorous brother took to horse and fled when that the Queen's officers came to take him, and he was found in a forest, with a good broad strong arrow deep between his shoulders, which some honest man, inspired thereto, had dexterously shot at him—for he was not stripped nor robbed, albeit his pockets were full and heavy with the gold and silver coins and objects which the mean felonious rascal had purloined from his trebly-injured brother.

This strange event was but a sort of bobbin

around which wound and gathered a thousand
threads and skeins of fancy until, ere long, the place
became populous with the airy inhabitants of my
own brain ; and they came and disported themselves at my bidding, and, as in the fabled tales
of old when nymphs and satyrs abounded in the
valleys, groves, and sylvan nooks, so now—as
became our Christian times and northern climes—
elves and fairies and sprights and gnomes and
witches and wizards and enchanters took their
place, and mingled with my mortals whom I did
invent—and many many a romantic story and hor-
rible catastrophe, and sweet idyl, and tales that
passed as dreams, and strange surprises, and noble
discourse, and sweet rencontres of love and
stratagem, and of poetry as of a better race of
women and men than lived in the common world.

I do but aver that what is most true when I say
that it had taken a dozen men, as swift and deft
writers as myself, to write down justly the half,
or the half of that half, of all the plays and tales
and poems and circumstances—the processions,
the changing scenes, the witty sayings, the
eloquent soliloquies, the fine and rippling dialogues,
the laughter, the tears, the indignations, sorrows,

wrongs, revenges, errors, kissings, rightings, and
many other things full of life and heart—and all
moving in a pure air and serene, as if everyone
therein had been alive, and had died out of the
mortal life into a spiritual condition which has
left corporeality not only far behind, but had
continued unbroken all the life below, but with
greater beauty, and freedom, and brightness.

And what then was I who was permitted to gaze
upon it all—to listen, to view, to admire, and laugh
and cry, and to shout with the victor, or gnash
my teeth at the villain, and rejoice when the true
love ran smooth again, and long to tell of the trick
and conspiracies that were a-brewing so that they
might be discomfited, and, in a word, be the one
spectator—but yet the all-sufficient audience ?

Who was I, William Shakspere, sitting there on
a gnarled tree-root, or lying on the sward, with
but the birds above which did furnish forth their
innocent and entrancing lays, and now and
again a soft splash as a fish leapt below, or a scurry
of some hare or rabbit that came on me surprised because I lay so still, and the buzz and hum
of bees, and the lisping of the river, the surging of
the wind in the trees—yea, and yea again, who

was I, this man lying there, with the eyes and ears that mortal had not borne before, to be allowed to sit there and peep undisturbed, and overhear without rebuke, and feel in every nerve and pulse of me all that passed, or to others would but seem to pass, but to me most assuredly did so, in this so full and active and glorious existence?

And also, asked I of my soul, are these things or the like universal, and is the world, in its fine ethereal elements, a life crowded with spirits and movements and emotions both sad and mirthful, and heroic or mean, and low and homely, and so much more than human in that they had ceased to be encumbered with the frameworks and shewings and trappings and instrumentalities of ordinary humanity—but that the common and coarse sense doth not perceive them, save only in a medley in their dreams, and save only when they are little children and so dream awaking as their fancies climb the slanting beams of holy light, and fill all the atmosphere with phantasy?

I could not answer to my liking.

Rather did I feel as if I had strayed where men are not allowed to wander and set foot, and that I had not been discovered.

And yet—'twas passing strange!—and yet I knew it was I who had invented them, and clothed them, and given them their parts and their exits and their entrances, their speeches, retorts, angers, loves, hates, jealousies, tyrranies, business, and all the trappings and the attributes, the work and the character and the conduct of it all ; and that I had but to wave my hand, or to will the thing, and they would all vanish, or come back, or mingle in many and other wise.

But this knowledge, of the which I did so often remind myself, did in no way or degree lessen my marvel and my ever fresh delight.

Sometimes came the thought, with a secret whisper to my soul's most inner ear, that I had strayed indeed in other and mysterious fashion, and that within this my body dwelt more than one spirit ; for I could not think that I, who would sometimes get drunk, and dance, and kiss the maids, and talk loose and lewd talk to the men, was all one with that other William Shakspere who writes of life and death and immortality, and of heroic moods and deeds, and of fairies, and dear lovers, and noble persons, and, in a word, of God and all his glorious wonders and splendours above, and demi-gods and men above and below, and of poesies and all the delicate fancies of the most fanciful mind on earth.

For, stay and understand. Had not I that thought, or that doubt, it were most insufferable vanity for me to write thus of myself—my whole and conglomerate self as men regard me. I were a coxcomb and a peacock and an ape, and like a silly empty-headed ploughboy, to speak thus of my personal self did I consider that I was but a single self, though compacted of many diverse elements of high and low quality and degree.

But I set down this my thought as the rather praising my co-inhabitant—the other William Shakspere who doth use me as his secretary. Or, if he be not a co-citizen with me in this corporeal residence—my mortal shape and frame— he is an honoured and a frequent guest. And if so it be that this my honoured guest is the Thomas of Utrecht whom I do so revere, my venerable and much-loved grandfather, than am I twice, and twice twice honoured above all men now or ever living.

I finished my historical play of HENRY THE VTH in, or about the month of November 1589*

* An obvious error.

and when the same was copied out fair and clean, which was a terrible work and a weary one, I once again journeyed to London, where, after some ado, I sold it to one Master William Sholton the brother of the man with whom I had once played for the sum of one thousand and Eighty pounds which was a great somme.

I paid my money at once to Silver Brothers to be at interest, and I took up my abode at the sign of the Pilgrims in Eastcheap—an Inn of good resort, near to the river and close to the Tower and the Coffeehouses of Cornhill and Lombard Street, and the theatre of Thomas* Sholton which was at Yeoman's Court near Cannon Street, close to the church† of St. Salvador the younger in Sherborne Lane.

I had engaged for to superintend the appearance of this play at its first ten performances, to instruct the players, to devise the dresses and the scenes, and to play the part of Pistol.

I had much difficulty in getting the proper men and boys to take the parts. Some would have none of this or of that, and others would only take

* See *Ante*.

† I reserve this interesting point for a later note.

the parts that another had: but at last, by the grace of God, and by the use of much patience and bad language, and much drinking and cajolery and railing, and, finally, of indifference and the devil-may-care—I-do-not airs, I completed the company, and we set about the learning of the parts and the preparations for the opening performance.

The dresses gave much trouble inasmuch as they were of so diverse, and eke possibly costly a kind, because the characters were, so many of them, nobles and knights, and high clerics, and mighty captains, and lofty ladies, and men at arms, and domestics of great houses, and had to be dressed in conformity to their state.

Likewise, the scenes were many, and of considerable variety, and had to be made, painted, and adjusted with much care.

Mr. Sellieres contracted for the Whole lot of the players, and would allow no man's or boy's name to appear except as a successive number of his own, to the intent that they be dependent on him alone, and also that they be not reached by others so as to get them from him.

The price contracted for, including himself but not me, was, by the week, £80—Eighty pounds—the which somme also comprised the Music, the money-takers, the checktakers, the men to keep order, the men to work the scenes, the men to light and snuff the candles, the dressers, call-boy, prompter, and all the men to appear as soldiers, servants, and the like, and the like. In short, everything except the cost of the candles and of the printing and handing about and showing the playbills.

My own wage as Pistol was £1. 6. 0. (one pound and six shillings) by the week, and I did receive nothing further for my instructing of the players and the general superintendence both before the production of the play and after the same, but I was at liberty to relinquish my part at any time after the first ten days, and to instruct a substitute at Mr. Sholton's charge for his wage.

The play was most successful from the very first night. There were many broken polls in the fights to get entrance.

The prices of the places were—

The boxes, of which there were 20, One pound the box to hold four.

The Pit, which would hold 225, One shilling for every person.

The back part of the Pit which would hold 100, Eightpence for every person.

The Galleries, which would hold about 400, Sixpence for every person.

There were also twenty seats upon the stage at Ten shillings for every person.

Altogether, when quite full the Theatre would hold in money £182. 10. 0. (One hundred & eighty two pounds 10 shillings.)*

The candles were esteemed to cost about eight pounds every night. The candle ends were the perquisite of the candle-men.

The Theatre was crowded suffocatingly every night, and I yielded my part of Pistol to one Mr. Sellieres N⁰ 20 :—and having no desire to tarry longer in London, I journeyed back to Stratford-on-Avon with the same wagon and horses, but not the same servants, as I did before.

Before I left London I had some merry times with my old friends—Ben Johnson, and the Englands, and Master George† Sholton, and Master Edward Sholton, and the Brothers Silver who invited me to dinner, where I met many famous men, to wit : Sir Walter Raleigh, and Sir Sholto Cavendish, and Sir Alfred Dare, and Lord North, and Sir Sydney Herbert, and Captain

---

* This seems incorrect.

† See *Ante*.

Drake, and Captain Frobisher, and Captain Stephen Stephenson, and Sir John Edwards, and Sir Showell Browne, and Sir Edmond Clowes, and Master Silver his Uncle, Sir Samuel Silver—a white-haired man of very reverend aspect, and of great affluence and generosity and learning: a man born in Germany, and a good and worthy Jew, who, with much wealth, had made right good scholars of his two sons at divers Universities.

These renowned and most distinguished men of so high degree had been gathered for that I meet them, and to do me honour.

I had timely warning, and did suitably array myself in a suit of black velvet, with point-lace for my ruffles and wrists, and silken hose, and a chain about my neck ; but other ornaments wore I none —except that the buckles of my shoes were of ebony and bright steel.

I bore myself modestly amid all the gracious things that were said, and likewise sung, of me, and there were who recited many excerpts from my plays, and I could scarce keep my eyes from flowing when I found myself at so great fame, and love, and pride of honest, and even noble, sort.

I tarried not in London for to go with the players to Windsor on the Queen's commands, to there perform the play, but I feigned me a fever, and so, with many gifts and many fond adieux, I, at length, departed—convoyed, as I was before by the Brothers England, my lusty as well as trusty friends, and my stout servants, and a cavalcade of good and gallant friends, full twenty five or more, who did ride with us to Enfield, where we held a grand carouse and then parted.

After a rest of some week's duration I resolved to make the most of my popularity, and of the popularity of the historical play, and so I without loss of time devised me the plot or plan of another on the like line of construction.

I accordingly, ere long, was once more at work in my accustomed place and manner, secluding myself as jealously as if I were a wizard in a cave, or a priest in a temple, or a threatened princess in a well-watched tower.

I began, as was my wont, by sketching out my plot and plan, and my characters and their work, and their chiefest speeches and discoursing and dialogues, with, perchance, here and there a few lines of verse, or a song, or a tournay of wits, or merry-andrewing of clowns, so as to furnish change and lighting of the great and more tragic or heroic portions of the play; as a painter doth portray the lights and shades with, at times, some touch of play, or simplicity, or sweetness, to heighten while it doth relieve the graver parts of the Picture.

As was my habit, or my humour, I made my working start by writing large on a sheet of paper with a brand new quill—

### HENRY THE VITH.

#### A TRAGEDY IN FIVE ACTS.

#### BY

#### WILLIAM SHAKSPERE.

I worked continuously at this play for the space of Six months, and I finished it on a Saturday eve, and I sent for a barber for to trim my hair and beard and moustachios, and I bathed, and changed every thread upon me, and then I made merry with my family and my servants and my friends and neighbours, as many as my house could hold, and many who had to sit in the other rooms, for the great room could not contain them all. I gave them of my best in house or shops that were in

Stratford-on-Avon, and I spared not purse nor pains, and the Curfew-bells did not abate our mirth, but we kept it up with song and dance, and merry toast, and much eating and drinkinge, until that the week was done and the Sunday morning was in the heavens, and about to descend to earth.

I copied out my play with my own hand, which took me over one month's hard toil, and weariness of head and hand and back: but I finished it at length, and a few weeks later saw me yet again in London, where I arrived on the 18th day of September 1592,—I being then about twenty eight yeares olde—and went straight to the same Lamb Inn in Eastcheap where the hoste, one Master Goodwyn, did give me my former chamber, and treated me with great and singular courtoisie and honneur.

After a night of refreshment and rest I sallied forth to see my friends before going to pursue my business.

Poor Ben Johnson was in very bad case, for he had grown fat, and very lazy, and very dirty, and very poor, and very drunken. He was lodging with a woman, one Mistress Jane Eyneshaw or Erneshaw, in Great Tower Street, and was in

debt to her in the matter of Six pounds or thereabout, and also owed divers sommes to other
people, the whole being of a total somme of over
twenty pounds ; and he was lost to the world,
and had parted with many of his bookes, the which,
when he told me thereof, went to my heart like
the stabs of a poignard :—and had not fit clothes
wherein to go abroad, and seemed deserted by the
world, and forgotten of all his friends.

I comforted the dear poor Poet and friend of my
heart, and I paid all his debts, and clothed him
anew from poll to heel, and twice at that for
convenience and change ; and I gave him twenty
more pounds for to go to another lodging, and find
and buy back his bookes if he could contrive to do
it, and to put himself in courage and in harness
again, and be worthy of his fame and of himself.
We did both get very drunk when we had settled
his affairs, and we had to send to the Englands for
to get us free from the Bridewell on Blackfriars—
the which they did, and laughed most monstrously at our plight, for Ben he could not walk
nor talk, but only grunted like a huge hog ; and I
was less overcome with sack and peppermint and
spruce, etc., than with fatigue in trying to hold

Ben up, and afterwards with sleep that seemed to wrap me round in many folds of thicknesse and voluptuous warmth and softness . . .

The Englands paid whatsoever charges and penalties were exacted (the which I did duly repay the next day) and took us away in chairs, and they told me, for I did remember nothing of it, that I did nothing but make rhymes and ballads and odes, and what not, all the way to the Lamb Inn; and belike I did, for they came easily to me at all such times, but I have no memory of what did happen then, or until I was awakened and helped to dress, about Eleven of the clock on the next day.

I sold my play to the same James* Sholton who had bought my play of Henry the Vth for One thousand & Eighty pounds, for he would not give me more, although, as I learned and for myself estimated, he had made a huge profit on my preceding play—at least two thousand pounds, after paying me—so that he had made that money and got my play besides.

I agreed to remain in London, as I did before, to help in the gathering and instruction of the players, and the scene painters, and the costume

* See *Ante*.

makers, and armourers, and other matters necessary for the production of the play ; and I
consented for a short time to play the part of
Bardolph at a wage by the week of £1 8/–.

It took three good anxious toilsome months
to get all in complete readiness for the first per-
formance at the Royal Theatre of Shows and Plays,
Eastcheap, which was the new name of Sholton's
Old Royal Tower Theatre, on the 8th day of
January 1593.

Master Sholton agreed with Mr. Sellieres to
furnish the entire Company, and all the servants
and attendants, as formerly set forth, except that
of the part of Bardolph, for the somme by the
week of Eighty-four pounds ten shillings.

The Theatre was designed to hold about 600
six hundred persons divided thus

| | | |
|---|---|---|
| In 20 boxes .. .. .. | 80 | persons. |
| In the Pit .. .. .. | 260 | ,, |
| In the Back of the Pit .. | 80 | ,, |
| In the Galleries .. .. | 250 | ,, |
| And on the Stage .. .. | 12 | ,, |

These various accomodations are of the money
value of £40 or thereabout*; which for six nights

* The computation is incorrect.

is £240; so that if to the aforesaid £84 - 10 - 0 be added the sum of Forty Eight pounds for candles, and a matter of two pounds 10 —ten shillings—for playbills, and the advertisements of the same in the coffee-houses and elsewhere, and if the receivings were only £200 by the week, there would be a goodly profit to Master Sholton—the which I never grudged him in my heart but, the rather, I rejoiced thereat.

The play was likewise exceedingly well received, and became a strong success from the very first night, and I was nigh surfeited with the honours which were heaped upon me—even when I simply walked in the street, and men said There goes Master Shakspere, and would smile, and doff their caps; and the women—and most chiefly they that were young and knew that they were comely—would smile, and glance, and send me many roguish and luring looks the which, for the most part, I would feign that I did not understand, and I would note their pretty poutings and at times, their disdaining angers.

I set not this down in coxcombry, but simply to show how well I had become known and liked to the people of London; for were I indeed a vain man, I would have repeated much that were indeed the act of a despicable and dishonourable wretch.

I made me all the haste I could to leave London, and to avoid as much meddling as possible with Master Sholton and his management of the play: and I feigned to be ill, and in need of rest, and such care as only my own wife and home could yield me; and so I quietly came away and returned me to Stratford-on-Avon, where I arrived all safe and sound on the 28th day of March 1593.

I lived very quietly for some weekes so that my tale in London might not be contradicted, and I heard from time to time that my Play was still the rage and the town's talk, and I was greatly pleased and proud thereat, and sometimes did regret my untimely flight from London, and sometimes did rejoice thereat, for I had no stomach for more roystering.

But, as often doth arrive when a man is too wise and over-discreet, I was trapped by my own innocent and well-intentioned stratagems, for divers of my friends, fearing for my health, did make up a company and journeyed down to Stratford-on-Avon for to visit me, and to cheer me in the illness which they believed I was in.

They came to my surprise and joy and consternation—Ben Johnson, and the Englands, and Thomas* Sholton, Sir Sidney Slattery, and Master Silver, and Sir Sholto Stoner, and Sir Edward Shorter, and some other of my fond friends.

I had not room enough in my poor house for so great and so noble a company, and all but Ben were lodged at the Saracen's Head, which was the chieftest Inn in Stratford-on-Avon.

I did confess my plan and subterfuge to them, and they laughed as if the very rafters were cracking, and methought more from their joy in finding me so hale and strong than from any wit in the thing itself. They were right loyal and good hearts, and I blessed God that he did give me such true friends—every man of them.

I made them welcome with all my heart, and with one or two, or it may be half a dozen right good men of my friends and neighbours of Stratford-on-Avon, we made merry, and held long and fierce carousal, and had games and sports and many pastimes for nigh a week on end.

One night we sallied forth, and half the town at our heels, and we heaved the Stocks into the

* See *Ante*.

river, and the constable was drunk and helped
us ; and we scattered largesse, and some did ring
a horrid peal, and all the women screamingly
laughed and clapped their hands, and all the men
and boys did cheer, and all the little children
were made exceeding glad, for we did gut the shops
of their sweetmeats and cakes, for the which we
payed whatever was demanded, and not an infant
that had not its entrails assailed by many potent
and, insiduous foes.

I look back on that mad time with composure,
and yet with astonishment. All damages were
quitted and made good, and nought but smiles
were seen in all the town. And, stranger still to
relate, not a man of all our Company, and not even
I, was one jot the worse in head, or stomach, or
in limb ; and when at length my beloved visitors
took to coach—though they had come in their
own—the town turned out and vociferously
cheered them on their way, and a score of us,
among whom was I, rode with them for nigh ten
miles to do them honour and to lengthen our
farewells.

I had, however, more need for rest after this
most happy and riotous embassade than even after

my labours in bringing to its public birth my last play—now so wondrously successful in London.

Amid all this that I have recounted, missing many episodes and glossing over many incidents, my mind was a-working as works the waterwheel while the Miller sleeps—yet in his Sleep dimly hears its movement as it mingles with the voices of the trees and air—and turns over and sleeps again ; or, as the charioteers left behind by break-downs on the road bear on their heads the harness and horse furniture of their foundered modes of travel while they walk to the nighest town or village ; or, as the Stag which bounds along the plain with its burden of antlers—the while it thinks of nothing but its fleetness of legs.

A plague upon the similes ! I am out of tune.

By odd times, in fragments, and as a joiner doth prepare for the house that is yet unbuilt, and store away each separate part of door and casement and lintel and carven baluster and other work, so did I, bit by bit, but not in any sequent order, get me ready for the writing of yet another play for the which, when once I did in reality begin, I already had a goodly store in notes, and even in completed portions, which I might use, or perfect, or turn to good account.

I once more equipped myself with a plenteous supply of material, and one fair morning I kissed my wife and told her that I was going on a journey all alone, and I pointed to my room where I used to work.

She knew my meaning, and sighed as she kissed me again, for she knew that expostulation were in vain ; for when I once was minded to write—I should the rather say, impelled by an irresistable compulsion from within—it was not money that now drove me to it, no, nor money that could now hold me from it.

I took me a sheet of paper, on which I wrote with a new quill

### *HENRY THE VTH, 2ND PART.

#### A

#### TRAGEDY IN FIVE ACTS.

#### BY

#### WILLIAM SHAKSPERE.

In this Play I desired and designed to carry on the history of the events during that stirring time of domestic war and dynastic struggle.

---

\* It will be perceived that there is much confusion of mind and memory in the following remarks.

The characters were mainly the same as in the first part, but the localities were different, and the chief points of interest were the Siege of Calais, trial of Joan of Arc, the Seizure of the throne of England by Henry the Vth, and the fight for the Crown by the Houses of York and Lancaster.

I also aimed to show that the condition of the nation was getting worse in consequence of these wars and unrests, and that there was a danger of England's relapsing into a province of France unless some peace were made of a definite nature, and the country allowed to recover itself by quietness and industry.

To this end I made my characters speak of peace, and of the fatal rivalries of the two Houses, and of the way in which the nation was being destroyed and impoverished.

I traced by the speeches of Rochester and Rowley how the land was being desolated, and all wealth eaten up, and all progress arrested ; and I led up, bit by bit, to my climax that the good of England required a strong ruler, and that Elizabeth was the Heaven-sent Queen to weld all the peoples, and to pacify all the factions, and to give the blessings of peace and plenty and liberty and progress to this England of our's.

I finished the play in January 1594, after six months incessant toil, and, having devoted a tedious month to fair copy the same, I hied me yet again to London, and this time I took my dear wife with me, for she never yet had been in London, and often had I promised her to take her with me on some fine occasion.

She was over-joyed, and I also was well-contented for many reasons—whereof I durst tell her of only some.

We lodged us with one Mistress Chomondeley at No. 27, Goldhawk Street in the Parish of Clerkenwell, and my wife was delighted with all the sights and wonders of the Town.

I sold this play to the same Thomas* Sholton for the somme of £1,080—One thousand and Eighty pounds—and engaged for to teach and learn the players, and to instruct the costume makers, and the scene painters, and makers of armour, and the like, and the like ; the all of which took me a goodly time.

My wife went nigh to being distracted and

* *Ante.*

insane with all the shops and shows, and all the honour and hospitality of many friends, and men of high estate, who did invite us, of whom I shall cite but a very few—

Master Silver.

Sir Francis Drake as he now became in his house at Colman Street.*

Master England.

Master Edward England.

Sir Edward Sholto.

Sir Thomas Everard Sholto.

Master Stephen Stephenson, the Queen's Secretary.

My lord Stamford,

and some more, at least a score.

She bought frocks and tuckers, and frills and fringes, and all the many objects, beyond a man's understanding and for a woman's fancied and imagined wants : and she glowed and gleamed, and was all over puckered and dimpled with her smiles, and the varied expressions of delight that a pretty woman can put on and off—if so it takes her whim : and she enjoyed her sojourn in London beyond descant or description.

* He is said to have had a house in Dowgate Hill.

The time at last arrived when all was ready, and the play was in due order presented to the world of London.

I took the part of Nym, but for ten nights only.

Master Sellieres as before contracted for all the parts, except only that of Nym, and to furnish the music, and all the service of every kind except the advertising of the play, for the sum of Eighty-six pounds by the weeke—leaving Master Sholton only the candles, and the printers, and the men who did take round the playbills to pay for.

For my part of Nym I was to be paid One pound 8 shillings by the weeke—the four days of my second weeke to be paid for at four shillings and eightpence for each night.

The play did not go so thunderously well as had gone its predecessors, but it went well enough.

All men said it was a great play and worthy of the classic writers, but I fear me the populace did find it somewhat heavy and dull, and above the level of their understandings ; and I did not, I think, sufficiently consider that men, and especially the ignorant, go to a theatre the rather to be amused, or terrified, or excited, or moved, than to be instructed.

Nevertheless, Sholton was doing a very profitable business, and was well contented, and I did receive vast praise from high and low ; and the Queen's Grace was pleased to send for me for me to read to her and her ladies and courtiers the parts where —— and —— discoursed, and also where the King soliloquised about sleep, and where Sir John Falstaffe had died and Dame Quickly described his death, at which the Queen did wipe her eyes and murmur, " poor Sir John ; and art thou indeed dead ? I could have better spared half a dozen of my real knights."

She gave me her royal hand to kiss, the which I gratefully and dutifully did, and she did also give me a guinea, and a gold and silver cup into which I could pour two flagons of wine—the which I did above six times on that same evening, when Ben Johnson and the Englands and some other of my most particular friends did come to see how I had fared at Court.

I had paid my money to the Brothers Silver for security and at Interest, and I had to go to them not once but several times for to get some for my purposes and for my wife's purchases.

On the 20th day of April 1594 we packed up

and loaded all on our wagon, with provisions, and cloaks and blankets, and arms, and we set out for Stratford-on-Avon—my wife now `full of fond ongings for home—and we had two stout fellows to be our guards, and the wagoner and his boy, who was likewise a burly dare-the-devil knave. I feared no man at close quarters, for I could wield my rapier as well as any cavalier, and better than most of them, having always kept up my fencing when I could do so.

As on former the like occasions I had an honourable and noble escort of good and gallant friends who, a goodly score or more, rode with us so far as Enfield, where we did part company after a rousing carouse and cheering the like whereof had scarce been heard in that place ; and in due time we reached to Stratford-on-Avon, where the town turned out to meet us, and convoy us to our house : for my repeated fame, and my being sent for by the Queen herself, had preceded me, and my townsmen were proud of themselves and of me.

I had cogitated much, beneath and behind and concurrently with all the bustle and the noise and the cheering and the money-making and the glorifying and the encomiums and the rest of it, that I must now write some plays of another hue. For I had written three great and solid historical plays, and I feared not only for my fame but also for my future gains, and, even more than for fame or pelf, for my genius, lest it might take on too engraftedly the style of thought, and purpose, and forms of speech, and all other the character and fixed phrases and channels of study and delineation and self-sameness.

I, therefore, resolved at this time to go out into another and entirely different direction—that is to say, Comedy and Poetry and Romance—altogether, and I devised a piece which should be a new shoot-off from the tragic style of my recent plays.

I thought out many plots and plans and, finally, I did choose one which mightily pleased my fancy, and the which I did compose and rehearse in parcels and fragments to myself when alone, in the woods, or in my chamber, and did often laugh so uproariously that my wife would come and ask me if I was unwell, or out of my mind, and my maids would be frightened for to come near the door.

At other times, I would walk abroad, and it was said that I did speak aloud, and mouth, and

sigh, and smile, and fling about my arms, until
that the older sort of people said that I was like
to my Grandfather Thomas, and the others did
believe that I was mad, or belike that I was drunk
—though divers of the staider sort did shake their
heads and say that William Shakspere was
inditing yet another new play, which would bring
him further renown—and much profit.

I got fuller and fuller with this my new play
and could not longer contain me, but was con-
strained to have delivery by pen and ink and
paper.

I took me a clean sheet and with a brand new
quill I wrote

## A WINTER'S TALE *

A

COMEDY IN THREE ACTS.

BY

WILLIAM SHAKSPERE.

I began this Comedy on the Eleventh day of
March 1595, and I worked upon it for nearly four
months, when I did re-copy it with my own hand,
and I went to London with one Master Seldon,
and one Master Shooter, both Citizens of Stratford-

* *Twelfth Night* is meant—See *further*.

on-Avon, who had occasion to journey thither upon a law-suit, and also for to buy some goods and merchandise for their several shops.

We went to the Lamb Inn in Eastcheap whereof the host was most hearty glad to see me again, as I had not stayed with him on my last journey by reason of my wife's company; and it was not long before that the news of my coming became bruited abroad and the house became full and roaring noisy with friends of mine, and with many who came from curiosity alone to see or to shake me by the hand, or to speak to me, but I never would drink or trink with strangers. I was ever courteous, but I eschewed all undue familiarity.

Many letters did also come to me from great men who did invite me to their houses or to revels, from traders and the like, and from Dames and love-sick damsels of whom there were not a few, but whom I treated better than they would treat themselves—for I forswore their tempting lures and cunning entanglements to dalliance and dishonourable pleasures : and I with most religious particularness did burn every missive and billet-doux, and oft got for my reward many a scowling glance and many a vengeful look—at the which I feigned to be all innocence and ignorance, and, if it pleased them better, all country-bred folly and thick-wittedness.

I sold my Comedy to Master Thomas Sholton for Eight hundred pounds and a royalty or rent of one pound for every night of its being performed in London or elsewhere, for the space of three years; and I agreed to instruct the players, and the costume makers, and the scene painters, and so on, and at last all was in readiness for the first performance—though we had much ado to get the players to learn their parts, because of the difference in the style of all the characters, and in the nationalities and manners.

We did at last surmount all the obstacles, and the playbills were put about in all the places of resort, and many smaller copies of the same were taken round and left at the houses of the Nobility and the Quality and the Aldermen and principal Merchants and lawyers and officers, and the like.

As with the Historical Tragedies so Master Sellieres did contract with Master Sholton for to man the entire play and to furnish all the attendants whatsoever, and the Music, for the somme of Eighty-six pounds by the weeke.

Master Sellieres, who had played the principal parts in the tragedies, played the part of Malvolio as if born in his very skin; and 'twas a marvel that he who had stormed, and looked terrific, and been magnificent and stately as King Henry the Vth, and as King Henry the IVth, and as Hamlet, should now strut and mince and mow as Malvolio, in such perfect guise that e'en my eyes ran with tears as I did laugh to see him.

The theatre rose at him as one man, and the shouts were so great that men ran from neighbouring streets to see what riot had broken forth.

I was right. The Town had had surfeit of ponderous plays and wanted relief in lighter tones and themes.

The play was a most stupendous success, and nightly they were forced to let no more people in and to refuse to take their money—the which was an inconsolable sorrow to Master Sholton.

I did not take my part in this play, and I hastened to leave London, after leaving my money with the Brothers Silver, the which I did very quietly on the 14th day of May 1595, and so returned to my home without any fuss or state, and resolved to rest apace.

I was at this time often ill of a pleurisy, and sent off to Warwicke fr a certain Mistress Jane Wadeing, a wise widow, who did make many wonderful cures. She very soon had me cured, and hale and sound, and I went about on my rambles in the woods, and the countrysides, as strong as ever I had been.

In these walks and rambles, with here and there a market, or a fair, or a wedding, or a wastrail of some sort or another, I yet did, in almost my own despite, fashion and hammer out on the anvil of my mind the plot or plan of yet another comedy ; and I soon gathered many a line, and many a figure, and many a quip, in readiness to weave them in my Cloth—when once I did begin, the which I did soon do, for the thoughts were bursting big within me.

On the 20th day of July 1595 I took to my room and with a brand new quill I did write on a great white sheet

## AS YOU LIKE IT.

**A**

**COMEDY IN THREE ACTS.**

**BY**

**WILLIAM SHAKSPERE.**

And I was, all the while I was a-writing it, like a bird caroling in a cage, nay, rather in a grove. My heart was as gay as was my fancy free, and my brain easy, pliant, fertile, generous.

The lines, the pages, the piles of pages, seemed to come as if summer winds had blown the rose-leaves off o'er-heavy flowers, and the air itself seemed redolent of all the scents of the wild woods, and vocal with all their sounds.

I never wrote anything in my life with so much joy, and with so little effort. Everything did seem to spring as from wells where all had lain ready and complete, and my hand did but seem the material instrument to set it free—and all too slow and cumbrous in its motion.

I durst not stop to read a page or e'en a part already written. I was ever thrust forward at a furious rate, and lost many a goodly line and phrase by my inability to overtake or keep up with the flow, as from some mysterious sourse beyond my influence or control.

When I could not go on writing for very weariness, from want of food or sleep, I still felt as if I were going on ; at my meals, which were but hasty mouthfuls, snatched almost at random, or in

my fitful sleep, wherein I would start at every few
minutes and jump from my bed and note down,
as on some imperative command, the thoughts
that kept tumbling o'er each other in their haste
to burst forth as from burning crater or an up-
rushing spring.

I had bethought me of the squire, in the guise of
a hermit woodman, whom I did once meet in
Arden Forest, as I think I did herein set out, and
on him did I build my Touchstone, but I had to
make him merry as well as wise, and philosophic
withal.

I do remember me going one day to the Forest,
and speaking nearly my play in solitude to the
trees around me; and it was as if all and every
character did move and breathe and live, and enter
and go out among the trees and copses as if it were
indeed a stage; and though some men may call me
foolish, or in fancy lost, I declare that I seemed not
to read or recite alone but that I heard each line,
and word, and speech, and dialogue, and grief,
and laugh, and sigh, and kiss, around and about me,
as, not the players, but the real embodiments of my
mind did utter or express them ; and that I, the
solitary spectator, did behold it all as if it had

sprung from some other source, or, the rather, were the real life indeed, and that I was privileged to be present and laugh and listen and applaud.

It was truly the dearest delight, and most subtle pleasure, the fashioning of the play—in the handiwork in which I seemed to have had so little share beyond the mere writing on the paper, and in the enjoyment of which I had such glorious zest.

When it was done I could scarce resolve upon myself to part with it, or scarce so much as to share the knowledge thereof with another; but that were folly, as I told myself in somewhat of this manner of argument :

*I.*—Now, Sirrah, what meaneth this nonsense of dallying with thy merchandise, to wit : thy new Play ?  Answer on the instant.

*W.S.*—I prithee, Master, have patience.  I do but dandle it a little longer on my knees before I do send it out upon the great world out-of-doors.

*I.*—'Tis folly, staring folly, I tell thee, and 'tis vanity, forebye.  For if it be so good a Play as thou dost fondly take it for, why, the world will say so too, and give thee honour, and money in store, and applause.

*W.S.*—Gently, good my Master. I know that what thou sayest is most true, but I did find it as an infant born of fairy mother in the Forest, and I brought it with me to my home, and did dress and fondle it, and am now grown so foolish fond thereof that I cannot lightly part with it, still less send it, in all its tender delicateness, among hard-hearted or cold-blooded strangers.

*I.*—I will have no more of such silly excusings. Thy mind, it misgives me, has become somewhat o'er wrought of late—most like because thou hast been too much alone, and wandering too solitary in the Forest, and thou art become a maudlin and most foolish man, and eke a conceited coxcomb.

*W.S.*—Enough, Sir. I shall brook this insolence of yours no longer. You are but a bare and sordid-minded pedlar. Here, take the Play, and be damned—and ne'er ask me to write you another. I will go and inveigh against you to the trees, my good respectful friends, and so—farewell.

Then I laughed, not displeased that I had thus served and helped to make up my mind, and I had a merry supper with my friends, and on the next day I set out for London, together, for my better safety, with one Master John Hargreaves of

Warwicke, who had occasion for to go to London on a matter of Account with a Company there.

I once more put up at the Lamb Inn, and on the very same day I sold my play to Master Edward Sholton and Master John Sholton in Co-partnership for the sum of Eight hundred and twenty six pounds, and a fee of One pound for every night when it might be performed in London, during five years.

They liked it so hugely that they did not lose one hour in seeing Master Sellieres who, when he had but read a few pages, became mightily inflamed with praise and satisfaction, and did march about the room with the pages in his hand and declaim—here a piece and there a piece—in his great voice, so that, ere long there was a crowd in the passage ways, and outside under the windows ; and someone passed the cry that it was William Shakspere's new comedy, and that Master Sellieres was a-sampling it, and there were loud cheers from the people outside the house, and eke inside the house, and Master Sellieres had to show himself and make his bow, while I did hide myself behind a casement.

But the people did so cry out for me that

Master John Sholton did make speech to them and
tell them that I was tired, being newly off a long
journey from Stratford-on-Avon ; and, being a
shrewd man, he did tell them also that he and
Master Edward had just bought the very finest
and most excellent Comedy that was ever written,
which would be shortly performed in public, and
he scattered largesse, the which was a clever, and
most stirring, and unforgettable advertisement.

And so I escaped, for I did not want to make
my bow from an Inn window to a crowd of idle
shouters, and the like.

It took but one month to prepare everything,
so much good heart did everybody put, each in
his degree or vocation, into his work ; and never
did players learn their parts, in action and movement and life-like similitude, as well as in mere
memory of words, with such celerity and hearti-
ness. The instructing of them was in itself a great
pleasure to them and to me, and when the costumes
were ready, and the scenery, we lost no time in
advertising the Town.

The scene was laid in my dear Forest of Arden.

As before, Master Sellieres had contracted for
all the players, music, and all the servants and

attendants, for the slump sum of Eighty-six pounds 10 shillings by the week, and as the Theatre was filled and over-flowed on every night, the Masters Sholton did most profitable business, and made money by the bucketful, as they say with us in the Midland County.

The Town was indeed most wondrously taken with the play, and I had the greatest difficulties to avoid being mobbed when I did appear in the streets, or surfeited into fevers by the invitations that I did daily receive. I left London for my home some twelve days after the first appearance of my play, well, and more than well contented.

I at that time made up my mind not to write another play for a long time to come, and I perforce needs write, then to confine my pen to fugitive pieces—such as poems or ballades, or little stories, and the like—and look after my affaires, the which had gone into some neglect.

I had some houses and lands, and interests in a ferry, and in divers other matters, being importuned into the same in my easy or over-occupied moments, inasmuch as all men knew that I had gotten large sums from my plays, and Rumour with her glib and numerous tongues had vastly enlarged the tally of the same. I also had lent right and left out of sheer softness and good-nature, without a dream of gain thereby, and I lost also left and right, besides bad blood, and scoffs, and ingratitudes without end.

I did my best to adjust much that was in dire confusion, and I employed one or several attorneys in cases where not alone my money but mine honour was at stake, for some did repay me with insolence and lies, or fictitous demands and counter claims, and I thought it only just to punish them: whereas I had bided the loss of the mere monies with philosophy and, perhaps, a laugh at my own credulities.

I did determine some degree of order, and was well pleased to find that I was possessed at that time, even if I did never earn another penny, of as much as might yield me about One Hundred and Ninety Pounds a year, besides the house that I did live in, and my chattels, horses, kine, and other items worth perhaps nigh to eight hundred pounds or more. Also, I had many and costly gifts in gold and silver, and many objects of great worth and curiosity, and stores of bookes—the which I prized more than all the rest.

I bought me more bookes in French and in Italian, the which tongue I found it most easy to learn, because I did well remember my Latin into which I was steeped and drenched and penetrated when I was the Under-Usher at Hoddingley ; and I was entranced with the bright and sunny and most passionate tales and romances in the which, methought, there lurked the makings of a play in almost every one of them, except them that were gross and too indecently indecorous to be so used.

Chiefly did I dwell upon, and read and read again until I did almost know by heart, the Decameron of one Boccacio, the Pencameron by the same writer, the Rabelais by a French writer named Montaigne,* the Stoics by one Stone, the Sybarite by the same Writer, the Science of Dramatization by one Peter Stowe of Salisbury, the Loves of Diana by Thomas Stone of London, the Loves of Venus by the same Writer, the Thesis of British Art by Master John Salisbury of London, the Loves of a Duchess by Stone, the Songs of a Warbler by Stephen Stephenson, the Songs of a Singer by the same poet, the Songs of The Seasons

* Obvious blunder.

by one Master Gregory of London, the Themes and Staves by Stone, the Poems of the Heart by the same, and others too many for enumeration.

I spent some months in a disorderly sort of fashion—reading, noting, writing odd bits and again, and completing none, and wandering about, mostly all alone, with a booke and my owne thoughts and fancies.

Yet all this seeming idleness and *sans méthode* were but cloaks designed to impose upon and deceive even my own self, for now and then, as if by stealth, I did get a peep into my own mind, wherein, like a close-guarded smithy, portions of what [might] hereafter be fitted into one whole play were being deftly fashioned, and laid aside for future use, when cooled sufficiently.

I was wont to smile when I, on tiptoe as it were, silently crept away, and to vow that I would come and smash the mouldings and the modelling and the forgings, and the hammered pieces: and yet I knew full [well] that, even while I vowed, I was thinking of some things that might complete, or harmonise, or fit in, the entire projection.

I fenced and fought and frowned and trifled for many months, the while I repeated, often most obstinately, that I would not commence another play—at least not yet for a lengthened while; and I began to fidget, and wax absent, and distraught, and fail to savour and to prosper on my meals, or to sleep soundly; and I often stopped and interrogated myself with great severity, and did exort and chide my ill and peevish and unaccountable humours.

But it was all in vain. I asked myself questions, which I knew full well were beside the mark, for to provoke the answers which I, in my secret mind, did equally know to be irrelevant and ingeniously hypocritical; and I made pretence to deem the conversation to be sincere. Then I would laugh at all this jugglery, and call myself many names of defamatory and wellnigh infamous quality, and I would swear lustily upon all imposters and crooked pretenders and feinants, and liers insly ambushes, and wearers of deluding masks; and perchance, go and seek out some good and willing soul and get drunk insanely.

But this thing could not go ever thus. There must come an end.

That end did come on the 18th day of December 1595 when I lost all patience and dropped suddenly all playing at hide-and-seek with my resolves and inclinations which did pull in diverse ways.

For I pushed aside my porringer at breakfast, and rushed into my own room as if I had been waiting in long suspense at the door thereof, and I violently seized upon a quill. I looked not to see whether it were new or no, and I did, with like impetuosity, pounce upon a large sheet of paper, and with eager and almost trembling hands, and hastening as if I feared to be frustrated in thus defying my determinations, I wrote

### THE MOOR OF VENICE.

#### A
#### TRAGEDY IN THREE ACTS.
#### BY
#### WILLIAM SHAKSPERE.

I did later alter the title to

### OTHELLO : THE MOOR OF VENICE.

I set to work as if I were in a fever, and as if I had been forcibly debarred from writing and were now but on sufferance, and for a very brief space of time.

I laboured on this play almost incessantly by night as well as by day. I gave myself neither respite nor rest, except for the hurried meals whereof I scarce tarried to know the nature, and often left untouched, or but half eaten; and the grudged hours of sleep—often on my elbows on my table, or on a couch in a corner of my room. I did not shave or stay to trim my moustachios and my beard, and I must have looked like a tarnished gnome, or newly unburied image, had anyone have forced or stolen access to me as I worked at that time.

I did intromet on Christmas Eve and Christmas day, but after that not at all, either for Lord's day or Saints' day, or Wife's day, or any day, until my work was done; and I did write with a flourish and devout thankfulness the words THE END, which was on the 3rd day of July 1596, when I curled myself upon my couch, and I did sleep until Sunday morning when the bells were ringing for the Morning Service. My wife had kept loving watch and care, and had kept me supplied with cushions and fresh air, and coverings, having first removed my shoon from off my feet and washed my hands and face most gently while I slept, and slept, and slept—over forty-three hours by the clock; and without a dream, and scarcely a single movement of my body or limbs.

I, in due time, was in London again with my play, which I had no difficulty in selling to the same Master Edward Sholton and Master John Sholton in Co-partnership for the somme of One thousand an eighty pounds, and a fee of One pound for every night when the play was performed in London, or in the Country towns, for the space of five years.

The Play was very successful from its very start. It came out in the same Royal Theatre of Shows & Plays in Eastcheap the which had by this time been enlarged so as to hold about a hundred more persons, chiefly in the Pit and in the Galleries.

The populace, and eke the Quality, were most mightily pleased with the Play, and every night, for about or above three months, the money that was refused had been welcome as the total receipts of more than one other house. I doubt not that I might have obtained better terms from other men, but I had dealt so long with the Sholtons, one or another, or in conjunction, that I had not the wish to go a-huckstering, and it would have savoured of dishonour, as I think, though others may be of a contrary and more worldly opinion.

It was I who named the price, and they did agree without bargaining or demur. I fixed the price on a calculation of the length of the play, but chiefly on an estimation of the time that it would probably be upon the stage, and the profits after payments of all outgoings, and I allowed amply for chances and uncertainties ; and of the residue so left in the estimation I did allocate for my price one third share, with an added sum for my expenses in London, and the many incidental outlays and spendings connected therewith.

I made no long stay in London, being fearful of my health, and I made pretence for to require to take the waters at Bath; but in reality, I wished to make my way to my home, the which I did almost by stealing away from London, after bidding farewell to but a handful of my intimates and most loved friends.

This time I did most savagely resolve to write no more, and to read the spritely and untiring demon within me a lesson of the grimmest, and show him which of us twain was the master— he or I.

I laughed merrily to myself as I pictured me his discomfiture if I embarked in trading—such

as in wools and hides and grain, and the like, as
did in a way my father Richard, and more
seriously, my grandfather Thomas, may God
grant him rest! and, much more seriously still,
my dear Uncle John, to whose dear memory I
breathe a loving sigh! and as do some of my
cousins of whom I have not made great allusion,
but whom I often met and entertained, and
counted in my every mention of my friends and
neighbours.

I also portrayed to myself the looks of surprise
and disbelief, or else belief in my sudden madness,
of the many men who did know me well if they saw
me in the Markets, or at a stall, chaffering and
chattering and shouting, and drinking and clink-
ing, and talking of nothing but shorthorns, and
winter lambs, and clips, and pelters, and corn and
barley, and so on, and so on, and so on.

I further made me a fancy sketch of William
Shakspere grown corpulent and coarse, and hail-
fellow with all men—mostly men of great and
breezy hands and breaths, of mighty tread and
heavy footfall, and brains whereof the scope and
span were scant and not beyond a market or a
getting the better in a trumpery commerce;

and I did not laugh with as much mirth and contentment as I did at first.

Nathless, I turned the heavy key in my lock, and imprisoned all my bookes, and I swaggered forth as a sort of man released from bonds and duly set at liberty to go and do whatever he listed, or to do nothing at all, if that better pleased him ; and I was like a young stallion in a meadow, who kicks up his heels, and runs races with himself, and rolls in delight, and neighs for very joy and strength of life.

It was very pleasant, and unrestricted, and wild, and irresponsible, and altogether most rollicking and gay for about a week ; and then, because I would not give [in] to the beseeching solicitation of my familiar for " just one book, gentle sir, may it please you—even a little and unimportant one," I began to peake and peck and pine at my meals, and in my bed, and at all times during the long and never ending day.

I have often thought that it must be a torment of the direst kind to take a refined and educated man, and lock him up, without books or pens and ink and paper, with people of a base and ignorant nature, and make him an enforced listener of their foolish, ribald, and most useless and offensive talk, day after day and month after month ; and that it were better to become mad outright.

I persisted for some days longer, and made believe to busy myself with divers occupations and pursuits, and some distractions, and gossips, and the like.

But soon all this palled upon my palate and, for that I would not yet give way, I was nigh brought to my bed with sickness, and for want of sleep, and diet, of which I had, thank God ! plenty—but could eat little, and enjoy none.

I, at last, rebelled or, the rather, I capitulated without a scrap of the honours of war, or any saving of my pride ; and never did lover rush more eagerly to his sweatheart's arms, or bird fly more devotedly to its fledglings in her nest, or captive run more passionately to his releasing door, than did I to my locked room and my ill-treated and imprisoned darlings which, gentle souls ! did not reproach me, but opened their fond bosoms to my hungry eyes.

I refreshed myself apace, and not to dwell too long on this, it was not many weeks before I had once again taken a grey goose-quill and written boldly

## THE MERCHANT OF VENICE.

### A

### TRAGEDY IN THREE ACTS

### BY

### WILLIAM SHAKSPERE.

I knew not well whether I should call it a Tragedy or a Comedy, so compounded of the two did it seem ; but I kept to the former designation, although the latter in many senses might not have been a-miss, or altogether inappropriate.

I was, at first, minded to make of Shylock a picture of my Grandfather Thomas—that is, to show the Jew in his true higher nature, before that oppression and wrong and derision and persecution and prejudice had made of him a hunted beast, and driven him to his wits for means to live, and to his deep-seated and most righteous resentments for means to get even when he could. I knew that the blood that flowed within me, and the brain that burned within, and the soul that felt and aspired beyond me, were of a Jew, and that I was a Jew—maybe, of longer and prouder and far purer descent of any vaunted peer or gentle in the land.

Also knew I well, for often had I studied the matter in Holy writ and in many writings of men, that, by nature, the Jew was a gallant warrior, a poet of the sublimest sort, a high-souled worshipper of God, and a gifted man above all other men in the whole categories of peoples in the world ; and it was marvellous to me that all the high-heaped degradations, and the cutting scorns that had been poured upon him—and the which were almost worse to bear by a noble race than heroic deaths, or barbaric exiles, or mean despoilations—had not broken his spirit or lessened his magnificent and disdainful pride ; and that he wore a magnanimous mind even when he had to bear insolent and foul shafts of enmity and opprobrium, shot at him by filthy hands, or cruel mocking lips.

But, on the other hand, I reflected that such a portraiture would not be understood or esteemed, in that it was so novel, and so little to the knowledge, or the taste, of the common herd, and eke their betters also.

I thought, too, that in my early years in London I had been called the little Jew, or the Jew boy, and hence that it would seem as if I wrote or preached upon a text whereof I was, myself, the chiefest part.

Nor was the further reflection absent from my business sense—and not perforce my Jewish sense, for that did all pull away from all considerations of gain, and was all for justice and truth—that I could never sell such a Play to any great advantage, and, perhaps, not even sell at all ; and that the populace would not endure it, for it would be counter to their conceptions. Nay, even that a great actor like Master Sellieres, or some others that I thought of, would refuse to act therein.

So, with many a sorrowful regret, and many a sigh, I addressed me to my task to make my Shylock so much of a Jew as might jump in with the general thought and conception of one, and yet with so much of what I could, without exciting question or opposition, say by or of him as might show that underneath his gabardine lay a noble heart—but soured by injustice and insult —and glad to read the moral. For I had intended, after all, and at the last, to make him magnanimous ; and when Bassano had bared his breast, and all the Court stood breathless, to throw down his knife with a bitter laugh, and to sweep grandly out—leaving them humbled and speechless with surprise.

For the tale from which I had usurped the scheme, or idea of the plot, and whether I did conform thereto or not, cared I not one damn.

But Portia did tempt me from this my intention —for the which I am, and ever shall be, sorry. For Shylock to triumph would appeal to noble minds which, alack! are few in number—and not often go to Eastcheap ; but for Portia to triumph in a game of fence, and jar and combat of wits, and redeem her lover—the which she could not do rattlingly, and in a gay canter, without a discomfiture of Shylock in the like proportion—light and shadow in perfect balance—and so I did ruefully sacrifice him to her—and the galleries.

I perfected the Play and, as was not my wont, I re-wrote a many page, and some more than once or twice ; and when all was done I could not but acknowledge that it was a fine piece of work, and would live for many a year after that I was in my grave ; and yet I felt stricken in my heart and in my conscience for the treason I had committed, and for the chances I had foregone. It did seem to my uneasy soul that my Grandfather Thomas looked at me with mutely reproachful eyes and sad countenance; and I vowed that if ever I should live to fifty years I would live long enough to right e'en these wrongs that I had done, and much more ; and that I would then write my greatest play, and champion the great cause of that noble and mysterious Race—the exiled darlings of a not ever-wrathful God—even if I should have to rent a theatre, and let in the populace for nothing.

So did I salve my conscience and give myself absolution ; and whispered to myself, behind my mind, that I was an impostor and a cheat ; and in due time was again in London with my play.

I had not delay or difficulty, but swiftly made my bargain of One thousand and Eighty pounds, and a fee as in the preceding matter, and gat me home again without staying to do more than help instruct the costume makers, and the scene painters, and read the play for one full day with Master Sellieres, who did then undertake to teach all the other players—for the which, and because of the curtailment of my sojourn in London, I did give him twenty guineas ; and I hastened away from Town, with John England and Edward England for to keep me company—poor Ben Johnson being then ill of another pleurisy.

I could not rest without seeing my play performed ; so I came up to London secretly on the 3rd day of Dec^re 1595, and I did put my cloak across my face, and paid my shilling, and took my place in the pit beside an honest citizen and his comely wife ; and there, with tingling blood, and thumping heart, and head aflame, did I witness it ; and no man of all who shouted and cried and swore and uttered loud encouragement to Bassano, and blessings upon Portia, and revilings upon Shylock, did suspect that the dark and silent little man in the Pit—whom the honest citizen did rebuke for a clod or a lout because he did not applaud when all the house did roar— was the author of that self-same play.

I came out at the end as if I had been glorified ; and also, strange to say, as if I had been sorely beaten. I felt elated, and most proud ; and yet I likewise felt humbled, penitent, and inexpressibly sorry, and more than half ashamed.

Then, as I walked along, and thought of my over One thousand pounds clear, I struck my forehead and said to myself with anger and

contempt—Why did I not cast it down and cry
Thy money perish with thee ?

But when I had supped and drunk a flacon of
rare Burgundy wine, I felt more comfortable in
my mind, and did console myself by calculating
that I yet had time to go to fifty years, and, in the
meanwhile, to write my greatest of all my plays,
so that, with the money I could earn from other
plays which I would write in the long months
and years between—as if in the intervals and vari-
ations of my work on that greatest play—I would
then be so rich that devil care whether I sold it
or not, or whether I admitted the populace at
smaller prices or none at all.

I told myself that I was satisfied, and that it
was a vow and a pledge, and I did drink to it—
and methought I caught myself a-winking to myself, and cried " peste ! Out upon thee, fool ! "—
and so to bed and sleep.

As secretly as I came so I did leave, and hie me
back to my home, a proud and, at times, a guilty
man, and an undiscovered traitor—until that re-
morse wore itself away in promises to myself, and
eke escuses, and lavish indignations and lamenta-
tions of the ignorance and prejudices of the mob.

I do not know for what price Master Sellieres did contract, but belike it was the same, or some trifling somme the less, as before.

I knew from what I saw, and heard from my friends and others, and from Master Sellieres, and Master John Sholton, that the play was mightily successful, and there was no abatement in the popular liking, or in the money-taking, after many months.

After a short time for repose and distraction, and the paying of some visits to friends in the towns of Warwicke, Burslem and elsewhere, I, without ado, plunged head foremost into a new work, the which I had been for some time considering, and shaping loosely in my mind.

I wrote on a brave large sheet the title thus

## A MIDSUMMER NIGHT'S DREAM.

A

COMEDY IN THREE ACTS.

BY

WILLIAM SHAKSPERE.

I had conceived this fancy in the Forest a long time ago—and had played or rehearsed it there a score or a hundred times, to myself alone, ere a